On behalf of the Board of Directors, officers and employees of Citizens Bank, we are pleased to present *Bay City Logbook, An Illustrated History*. We extend our sincere thanks to the author, the Historical Society of Bay County and the many people who helped make this book possible

Citizens Bank is proud to play a role in Bay City's current development. It is with special pride that we bring you this handsome volume. We hope it will be a valuable addition to your family library and a collector's item in the years to come.

The Stuart S. Young Grocery at 323 Adams in 1904.

Mr. and Mrs. Charles Stephenson Store at 13th and Fraser.

BAY CITY LOGBOOK
An Illustrated History

by
Jeremy W. Kilar

with
Ronald Bloomfield
Bay County Historical Society

G. Bradley Publishing, Inc.
St. Louis, Missouri 63131

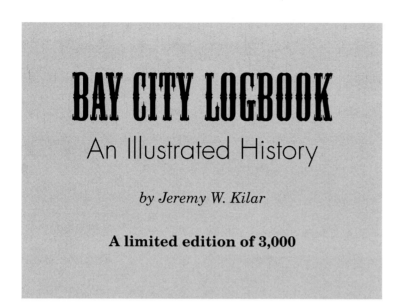

BAY CITY LOGBOOK
An Illustrated History

by Jeremy W. Kilar

A limited edition of 3,000

PUBLICATION STAFF:
Author: Jeremy W. Kilar
Coordinator: Ron Bloomfield
Copy Editor: Lois Honsowetz
Cover Artist: John McCormick
Book Design: Diane Kramer
Photo Editor: Michael Bruner
Publisher: G. Bradley Publishing
Sponsor: Citizens Bank

Published in cooperation with the Bay County Historical Society

Note: Photographs used on the front and back end pages were taken from the extensive files of the Historical Museum of Bay County. The photos were selected for their visual interest and, although from Bay City and the area, many are unidentified.

Making some final changes during production are, left to right, cover artist John McCormick, author Jeremy Kilar, and coodinator Ron Bloomfield.

© Copyright 1996 by G. Bradley Publishing, Inc. All rights reserved. Printed in the United States of America. No part of this publication may be reproduced, stored in a retrieval system, or transmitted, in any form or by any means, electronic, mechanical, photocopying, recording, or otherwise without the prior permission of the publisher.

ISBN-0-943963-57-5
PRINTED IN THE UNITED STATES OF AMERICA

Table of Contents

Author's Preface 10

Chapter 1: First Inhabitants 11

Chapter 2: "Lower Saginaw" 20

Chapter 3: Lumbertown Enterprise 34

Chapter 4: Lumbertown Life 56

Chapter 5: Lumbertown Legacy 85

Chapter 6: Bay City Logs On 130

Chapter 7: Wars, Depression, and Prosperity 166

Chapter 8: Determined Durability 189

Acknowledgements, Contributors 203

Bibliography 204

Index 205

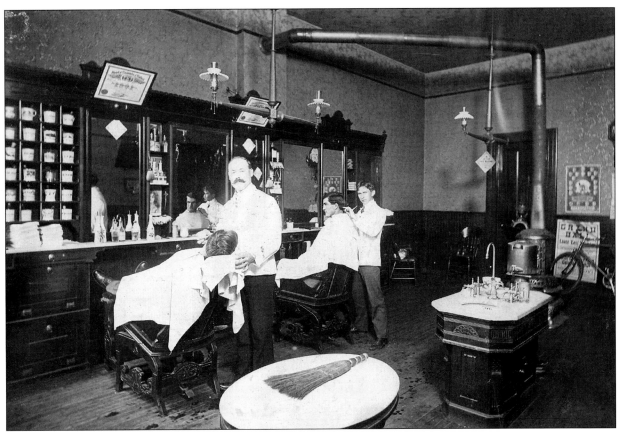

Joe's Barber Shop, circa 1901.

The Bay County Historical Society

The effort to preserve Bay County's rich history dates back to New Year's day, 1874, when a group of pioneers met at the Fraser House Hotel. At this meeting, the Bay County Pioneer Society was formed, with well-known names like Israel Catlin, Curtis Munger and Albert Miller helping to direct activities. Later that year, Albert Miller became the first president of the Michigan Pioneer Society, and Bay County started to preserve its own heritage, and to play a large role in writing the history of Michigan. The Bay County Pioneer Society lasted only about 15 years, but the memoirs of many of its members ended up in the Michigan Pioneer and Historical Collections, one of the richest sources of pioneer history for the State of Michigan.

The present day Bay County Historical Society dates back to 1919. A meeting was held by the Bay City Women's Club in May of that year to create interest in organizing a local historical society. The Bay County Historical Society was organized with the purpose of encouraging historical study and research, collecting and preserving materials relating to the history of Bay County, and encouraging programs that would stimulate interest in local and state history. With that start over 75 years ago, the Society began its dedication to preserving and telling the story of Bay County history.

The first space occupied by the Society was a few display cases in the corridors of Central High School. George E. Butterfield, charter member of the Society, supervised these cases. Mr. Butterfield was a teacher at Central High during part of this time, and later became the Dean of Bay City Junior College. His guidance and devotion was one of the major factors to shape this growing Historical Society, and his legacy would be carried on through the dedication of his son, Judge Ira W. Butterfield who practically grew up with the Society. The Butterfield Memorial Research Library was dedicated to their honor in 1995.

During 1934, the Society opened new quarters in the recently built Bay County Building. Their area on the second floor offered exhibit, storage and work space. An appropriation of $200 by the County Board of Supervisors allowed for personnel to supervise the new museum. Many still remember the County Building museum, with its rows of exhibit cases overflowing with objects of historical interest to the visitor. Small handwritten labels identified the "old knife", "old shoe", "old button hook", and "old teacup" for the patron to see. Almost everything in the

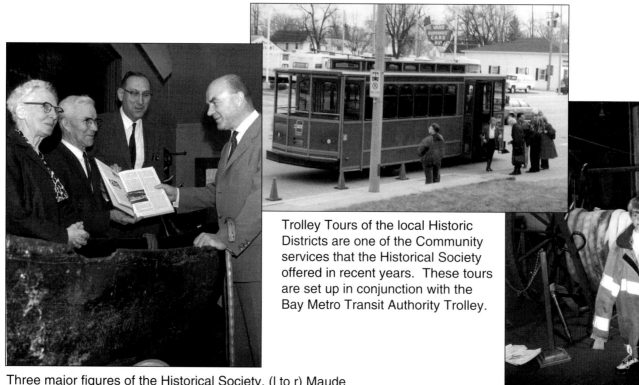

Three major figures of the Historical Society, (l to r) Maude Greenman (long-time Museum Curator), George Butterfield and Dr. Louis Doll (Former Society President) present a copy of George Butterfield's Bay County Past and Present to the Mayor of Ansbach, Germany, Bay City's sister city. In the foreground is the "dugout" canoe many people remember seeing on display in the County Building Museum rooms. The photo is dated July 3, 1962.

Trolley Tours of the local Historic Districts are one of the Community services that the Historical Society offered in recent years. These tours are set up in conjunction with the Bay Metro Transit Authority Trolley.

Programs such as gallery tours and educational activities get the public involved in local history. Many of these programs enlist help from around the community. Here a student enjoys a "hands-on" learning experience during a spring program on firefighting which the Historical Society executed with help from the Bay City Fire Department.

Society's holdings were on display, and the more to see, the better.

The Society continued to receive donations of items from a community devoted to the preservation of their heritage, but the temporary spaces found to store materials soon overflowed. During the early 1960s, the now very cramped rooms in the County Building were needed by the newly reorganized Court System and the Historical Society was asked to move. By mid 1968, the Society closed its doors in the County Building and set about re-locating to a site at Center and Hampton Streets. The board had purchased the house and property from the Diebel sisters, for a new museum. The funding came from the Bay City Schools, the County and private donations.

In 1970, the new museum on Center Avenue became the Museum of the Great Lakes, sponsored by the Bay County Historical Society. This new name brought about a more regional focus and exhibits strove to interpret the Great Lakes region, not just Bay County. Part time employees became professional staff, up to date with the current thinking of the museum profession; however, volunteers still made up the bulk of the manpower. The countless hours of dedicated work finally came to fruition as the Society became more a part of the community it served.

Still, the holdings of the Society grew and storage was increasingly becoming a problem. In the early 1980s, it was decided that another place was needed to house the Society. The plan, this time, was to acquire a place where everything could be housed under one roof. The former National Guard Armory was offered, chosen and renovated for the Society. This building offered significant benefits: its location was good, it was large and it was an historic building. The initial renovations were complete and the Museum opened for business in 1988, and permanent exhibits soon followed. During this time, a few millages helped provide the operating support for the Society, but in 1995 a 20 year millage assured the continued commitment of the community to the mission of the Historical Society.

Today, the Historical Museum of Bay County continues to provide for the preservation and interpretation of the unique heritage of Bay County. Although the name was restored to the Historical Museum of Bay County in the early 1980s, the Museum continues to serve a larger audience, drawing visitors and research requests from all over the world. On the local level, historic preservation within the community has the Society playing an active role in community development. Bay County has a rich and unique heritage and should be proud to have an Historical Society and so many dedicated volunteers that have enjoyed over 75 years of commitment to preserving that legacy.

R.W.B.

The County Building rooms. Almost everything was on display. Pictured in second photo is Betty Sporman, Curator.

The 1700 Center Avenue Stage. The Museum of the Great Lakes developed in this converted house.

The Armory quarters, 321 Washington Avenue. This building allows all of the Historical Society collections to be gathered under one roof and provides the largest exhibit area of any prior building.

Author's Preface

The title, *Bay City Logbook,* suggests several historical themes that are interwoven within Bay City's past. Indeed a "Logbook" is a record of events most commonly associated with a ship or aircraft. From that perspective, the community's ship-building industry, its fishing lore, and its pioneers in aviation legitimize the title choice. More recognizable, though, is the reality that little progress would have taken place had it not been for the city's original dependence on logs and lumber. The lumber boom of the second half of the nineteenth century initiated the development of a complex urban society. Economic guideposts put in place during the lumber era also directed the city along the twentieth-century highway that continues the community's industrial journey. A "Logbook," in the broadest sense of the meaning, is "a record of progress of a journey or an experiment." This defines Bay City's past well, and gives direction to an illustrated history that traces both the pathways to progress and the innovation that characterized Bay City's heritage.

A logbook's author will often begin his journey with several short but pointed introductory notes scribbled on an inside cover. These serve as a reminder to pay special attention to particular themes, events, people, and trends that the author anticipates will be crucial in evaluating the success of his journey or experiment. Such is the case in setting up Bay City's Logbook. There are definite historical events and trends that clearly mark Bay City's past as well as its present. Truly, "past is prologue" in Bay City.

While perusing *Bay City Logbook,* the reader must keep in mind that the community was originally a "booster" town, or "paper city," where land and lots were sold in all-out competition. Initial prosperity was very limited and the community failed to acquire a deeply-rooted entrepreneurial class, but natural geographical advantages—pine trees, rivers, and the Saginaw Bay—foretold inevitable success. Between 1870 and 1890, location enabled Bay City to become one of three leading lumber ports in the nation along with Saginaw and Muskegon. Bay City had several of the world's largest sawmills and developed as a core community serving a large regional area. These sawmills needed workers, and soon large, persistent, and diverse ethnic communities settled within rather specific neighborhood enclaves. Bay City's immigrant workers—Germans, French, Poles, Swedes, and Irish—often brought in by absentee lumber barons as strike breakers, maintained an uneasy relationship with the community's lumbermen. The conflict-ridden "Great Strike in the Valley" in 1885 exacerbated these uncomfortable relations and created class and ethnic divisions that were to persist into the next century.

Amid the boom, the trees suddenly ran out, and quickly Bay City's large, absentee-owned sawmills were shuttered and abandoned for greener forest in the West. Although hindered by the lack of dynamic entrepreneurial leadership at the turn of the century, the city's diversification into hardwood manufacturing enabled it to progress into the twentieth century. The nearby automobile industry soon sped up local economic development. Though slow to develop heavy industry, several auto-related manufacturers and nearby industries let Bay City settle into a comfortable and rather durable existence. Its pleasant streets, active business communities, neighborhoods, and strong ethnic enclaves gave the city character and a stamp of contented livability.

When Bay County celebrated its centennial in 1957, the community was in its heyday. Its population reached nearly 57,000 people. Prosperity reigned for another decade; however by the 1970's the up and down fluctuations of the auto industry and the outmoded industrial base began to take their toll. Major manufacturers closed and the city's population slipped to less than 40,000 in 1990.

Yet as the years passed, Bay City was able to endure. It maintained a viable downtown and diversified into a regional retail marketplace. While the bawdy saloon districts of the lumber era are gone, the West Side developed as a regional center for evening entertainment. Neighborhoods persisted and generation after generation continued to identify with local churches and schools. Partially a bedroom community where a good many people work outside of the city, the community endured because it continued to provide a haven for social and cultural diversity that remained interesting and attractive to a good many residents.

These are the themes that direct Bay City's past and should be noted as one looks through this illustrated history. By combining text, remembrances, and narrative with photographs, the reader can grasp the legacy of Bay City's enduring past. It is a journey marked by persistence and durability. *Bay City Logbook* should encourage everyone to study the community's past as an indispensable resource to plan for the future.

The blending of cultures. Indian guide, Chief Shoppenogons, with hunter, c. 1890.

J. W. K.

CHAPTER 1: FIRST INHABITANTS

> *One of the most perplexing of great American mysteries: Who were the Mound Builders? Skeletons unearthed in Bay City show characteristics differing from later Indians! Pottery and implements found indicate a more advanced culture and civilization. Where did they come from?*
> *Bay City Times, Centennial Edition, June 16, 1957*

ANCIENT INDIAN CULTURES: THE MOUNDBUILDERS

The Native American culture that archaeologists call the Moundbuilders remains one of the best kept secrets within the study of regional history. As late as 1957, local and regional historians were unconvinced that a powerful and artistically accomplished civilization once flourished right in their own backyards where the ruins often lie.

The most obvious evidence of this past culture—cone-shaped mounds ten to twenty feet in diameter and height—was well known 150 years ago. However, few seemed to believe that these burial sites, richly laden with silver, copper, stone, clay, and shell artifacts, were the products of a remarkable, prehistoric culture of Native Americans. By the late 1880s, archaeologists were beginning to unravel the mystery of the "ancient moundbuilders." Indeed, at the turn of the century it became accepted by archaeologists that the mounds—several were scattered within Bay City's city limits—were built by the ancestors of the Midwestern Native Americans.

Unfortunately, much of this archaeological evidence remained unknown or unacceptable to local historians. To many, the Moundbuilders had clearly lived long before Columbus. It was assumed, there-

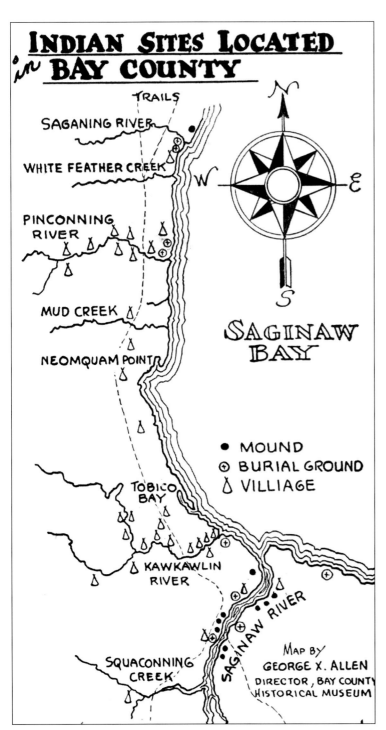

Map showing early Indian villages, mounds and burial ground sites in Bay County.

There were nearly a dozen Hopewell burial mounds, similar to these, located along the Saginaw River in Bay County.

fore, that the Indians present at the time of white contact—the Ojibwa, Ottawa, or Potawatomi—were incapable of producing these mounds or the fine works of art found within them. Various nineteenth-century theories ascribed construction of the mounds to a vanished race, the Vikings, Indian "Hindoos," or extinct civilizations from Mexico.

When the myth was exposed, it became accepted among scholars that specific Woodland cultures, the Hopewell Indians (ca. 600 B. C.-800 A. D.) of southern Ohio and the Mississippian Indians of southern Illinois (800-1400 A. D.) built the mounds. Ethnocentric European settlers were nonetheless slow to dispense with the myth of a vanished race. The destruction of vast numbers of Native American peoples in the late nineteenth century was more easily accepted if settlers could rationalize that they were merely wiping out a violent and inferior race that had earlier destroyed the noble Moundbuilders. The myth of the Moundbuilders was slow to die. Who were these ancient ancestors of the Native American Indian?

THE FIRST PEOPLE CHANGE THE SAGINAW BAY AREA

Recent historical interpretations have placed the Native American within the mainstream of this country's history. The willingness to acknowledge the historical significance of Indian cultures, coupled with hundreds of archaeological digs employing modern technologies, has led to a revolution in the interpretation and understanding of ancient cultures. Conclusions drawn as little as thirty years ago are today outmoded. And a good deal of the evidence that led to these new beliefs has been gathered within Bay County and along the Saginaw River.

Several important facts stand out as a result of recent discoveries: *There were* ancient Paleoindian (12,000-8,000 B. C.) people in Bay County. Moreover, climate changes made them and their successors, the Archaic cultures (8000-1000 B. C.), extremely mobile and adaptable to their environment. Likewise, these ancient peoples left a physical historical record, and they did not necessarily live in perfect harmony with nature. Early humans markedly changed the land and the waterways upon which they lived. Lastly, Woodland cultures (1000 B. C.-1600 A. D.), prior to white settlement, created an advanced civilization that was far different from the stereotype of primitive, nomadic, cave-dwelling tribes of hunters we envision today; and, most important, the link between these cultures and their descendants—the Ojibwa and Ottawa—is rapidly being established.

The Paleoindians appeared from a southern migration route around 12,000 B. C. when the last glacier receded. Extensive forest cover and a cool climate allowed several big game species—caribou, giant beavers, sloths, elk, and horses—to thrive. Although Paleoindian sites are rare, since the people were nomadic and carried few possessions, their distinct fluted spear points have been found in Bay County. Paleoindians often used these points to hunt large mastodons that populated the southern half of the state. They slaughtered the mastodon and stored its meat in cool bogs or spring-fed ponds.

By about 8000 B. C., Paleoindian cultures disappeared or were absorbed by the Archaic cultures. These Indians were also hunters and used several varieties of stone spear points; they also made copper tools and ornaments—hence the name "Copper culture." Woodworking tools and burning enabled them to construct dugout canoes. These vessels permitted

Fragments of mastodons' have been found near Bay County. Mastodons were hunted by Paleoindians and their meat stored in spring-fed bogs and ponds. A mastodon was about the size of a present-day African elephant.

the Archaic peoples to roam the entire Saginaw River and its tributaries and to establish a number of hunting and fishing villages along the river and bay.

The gradual warming of the Great Lakes led to the first permanent Indian settlements along the Saginaw River around 3000 B. C. Although their villages were not large—perhaps 50 to 60 people—these Later Archaic peoples for the first time began to strike a balance between utilizing animal and plant food sources for subsistence. This is the first evidence of "regional adaptation." The bay area provided sufficient ecological diversity and easy water transportation that permitted native populations to increase and develop new technologies.

Most excavated Later Archaic sites (3000 to 1000 B. C.) are burial sites. Several along the Saginaw reveal fire pits where plant and animal remains define a subsistence existence based on summer fishing/gathering and winter hunting. Fish bone remains along with copper hooks, gorges, harpoon points, and gaffs show that fish were gathered in the spring during the spawning season. In the summer and early fall, hunting and gathering along the Saginaw Bay provided wild rice and small game.

Recent archaeological evidence also suggests that Late Archaic cultures may have altered their environments by impounding fish with earthen dikes or burning the forests to drive game and improve the harvest. These activities increased river and bay run-off and lowered water quality. Archaic cultures transformed their river landscape in order to make use of the natural resources available along the Saginaw Bay.

Though the Late Archaic peoples disappeared around 1000 B. C., the "Early Woodland" cultures (1000 - 300 B. C.) that succeeded them were only slightly different. Around 300 B. C., "Middle Woodland," or the "Hopewell Indians," began to leave evidence that they had become the dominant culture in the region. It was the Hopewell who built most of the mounds found scattered along the Saginaw River. These Indians entered the Great Lakes from southern Ohio and Illinois, displacing the few remaining Early Woodland peoples.

Approximately 28 Hopewell villages were located along the Saginaw River. Excavated mounds were found at 24th and 22nd streets near Water Street and the river; on the West Side at State and Marquette; on Linn Street; and along Midland Street and Salzburg. Archaeological evidence suggests that between 200 B. C. and 1000 A. D. these inhabitants gradually made the transition from a primary hunting/fishing/gathering existence to one dependent on semi-domesticated and domesticated plants. From 300 B. C. to 350 A. D. the average temperatures were warmer than today, and the climate change furthered agricultural development. A line across the state, roughly from Bay City to Muskegon, represented the northern limit where 140 frost-free growing days occurred for reliable agricultural production.

In the Saginaw Bay area by 1000 A. D., the Hopewell Indians developed four basic subsistence patterns: primitive agriculture, hunting, fishing, and gathering. In pursuit of these livelihoods, the Woodland tribes altered the face of the Saginaw River and bay by using limited technology to increase agricultural, forest, and aquatic food resources. Pioneer white settlers often failed to comprehend the complex food cycle of these Natives. On their later arrival, settlers assumed that they had come upon a natural, untouched wilderness inhabited by primitive gatherers and hunters. Early white settlers did not

Corn changed Native cultures by providing more time to develop skills and new technologies. Indian women and children chased birds away from the corn fields.

understand the length of time the Indians had existed along the bay, or that human occupation for any long period materially affects the soil, water, flora, fauna, and even the climate.

The first subsistence pattern appeared in the southern reaches of the Saginaw Bay area where people depended on domestication of corn, sunflowers, beans, and squashes for their livelihood. As early as 500 B.C. inhabitants at Greenpoint, where the Tittabawassee converges with the Saginaw, cultivated a type of squash. The rich bottomlands along the river eventually paved the way for more efficient use of plants and a gradual decline in hunting as a primary food source. A survey of plant remains at various sites along the bay reveals that all of the major crops used by the Hopewell arrived here by 1000 A.D. The Hopewell also were the first to manufacture pottery on a large scale and use it for cooking.

The shift from hunting/gathering enabled the Native populations to increase and for long-term, year-'round settlements to develop. County burial sites discovered in the last decades have led archaeologists to believe that a few large villages contained well over 100 inhabitants and spread out over 15 to 20 acres. Perhaps as many as 3,000 Indians lived along the Saginaw. In each village there were 10 to 20 scattered wigwams—round-shaped, single-family dwellings with dome shaped roofs made of saplings covered with bark or hides. The Hopewell located these villages quite carefully. They needed safe and convenient beaches for their dugouts, and they wanted easy access to local supplies of fish and waterfowl.

The second major economic adaptation by Woodland cultures was based on hunting. Dependent on moose, caribou, deer, elk, and bear from the forests in the winter, the Natives often sought small game—turkey, beaver, partridge, and geese—along the river in fall. In the winter months village bands broke into family hunting clans and relocated in the forest away from the cold lake winds. In the spring they returned to the Saginaw Bay for fishing, gathering, and planting.

Fishing was the third subsistence pattern and of course very important to these inland shore fishermen of the bay. Over 20 species of fish bones have been discovered in various sites along the Saginaw. A thousand years ago the Saginaw was a slow-moving, relatively clean and cool river. The bay began to be slightly darkened by run-off and aquatic vegetation. Fish from these waters supplied 25 to 30 percent of the Indians' food and compelled them to develop a variety of fishing methods. During the spring spawning period, high waters carried large numbers of fish into backwater ponds. There the Natives impounded the fish in man-made sloughs, ponds, and marshy flood plains. Fish could be stored for long periods of time in the ponds and later harvested and dried, smoked, or frozen in large numbers. Nets, clubs, spears, and baskets were used to collect fish.

While the Indians' fishing practices did not turn the Saginaw Bay into a polluted waterway, their methods altered the ecology of the river's mouth. Repeated and extensive flooding of low-lying lands killed vegetation. Like their burning practices for farming, flooding cleared forested areas drove larger game inland, and silted the river and bay. Anthropologists have now come to believe that Native impounding and flooding along the bay, not burning, significantly altered the Saginaw basin and nearby forests.

Fires were often used over much of the region to improve the fourth subsistence pattern—gathering. The most important spring activity was the gathering of sap from maple trees for sugar. In May, the Natives collected cattails, pepperroots, wild leeks, and swamp milkweed. In late June, they picked the groundnut, a small potato-like tuber that flourished in the region's damp soil. Great quantities grew around the bay and

Hunting was always a primary occupation of the Ojibwa in the Great Lakes. This scene depicts muskrat-spearing in winter in the 1870s.

In addition to agriculture and hunting, gathering was the third means of Native subsistence. Here the Ojibwa gather rice by beating grains from rice stalks in the shallows.

especially near "Pinconning" (or "place of the pin," or "wild potato"). In late summer and fall, they gathered wild rice, which was the Hopewell's most important crop before they grew corn. Richard Yarnell, an expert on Woodland food sources, listed 130 plants used by the Hopewell for food.

The Indians set fire to wooded areas and marshes to increase vegetation growth, to improve travel and visibility, and to drive game. Light burning would keep down seedlings and thin the forest. Forest thinning increased the production of nuts, berries, and maple sap. Heavy burning of the marshes and forests opened the land for farming and drove large game into the woods. Open fields were also burned to encourage special wild crops and replenish depleted soil. Hunting became less important as agriculture and gathering became more developed.

Burned-over forests and marshlands gradually changed the nature of vegetation and fish species in and around the Saginaw Bay. Fire-ravaged land, while improving agriculture, also increased sedimentation in the river and bay during spring floods. The depth of the river and the mouth of the bay changed, and sediment and vegetation warmed the waters and drove away certain species of fish. Lake trout and smallmouth bass became less frequent spawners in the murky waters; drum and catfish remains indicate that these species became more common in the Indians' diet.

Agriculture was the ideal pattern of subsistence. The overriding quest of these Hopewellian peoples was to develop a storable food surplus that could be used in times of scarcity. Corn was the ideal crop for it was high in energy and could be easily stored. Hunting became less secure as the forest grew tall and the lack of underbrush dispersed big game. Fishing and gathering supplanted farming during cool eras or periods when high waters flooded the rich bottomlands. Well into the period of white contact, despite modern tools and seeds, Natives continued to procure food in traditional ways. They altered the land and the river as they had for centuries; and what is known today is that these Woodland Indians were far from a simple people controlled by their environment. They shaped Bay County and made it what it was when the first white man arrived.

One method of controlled burning was to fell a tree by burning and continuous scraping.

Maple sap is being collected here at an Ojibwa sugar camp. The sap was later boiled on an open fire to produce sugar.

THE "FIRST PEOPLE"

After 1200 A. D., there was a period of significant cooling in the Great Lakes area, climaxing with the so-called "Little Ice Age" about 1695. This accounts in part for a decline in agriculture and a dispersal of the Indian populations from around the Saginaw Bay shortly before the white man settled along the river. The descendants of the Hopewell peoples called themselves the "Anishnabeg" or "the first people." These "Late Woodland" people, thought to have migrated into the bay from the north, were not linked until recently to the earlier Hopewellian cultures. However, archaeological excavations of burial sites — including several along the Saginaw — have connected the Anishnabeg to earlier cultures. Analysis, especially of tools, weapons, and trade goods and of the physical characteristics of the dead in later Anishnabeg burial mounds, shows similarities in arrangement, detail, and appearance to earlier Hopewell. Today we are more assured that there indeed was a link between the ancient Moundbuilders and their descendants — the Anishnabeg.

By the time of white settlement in Michigan, 1674, "the first people" had split into three tribal groups: the Ojibwa, the Ottawa, and the Potawatomi. All three periodically were in the Saginaw Bay area. The change from a subsistence existence to dependence on the white man's goods exchanged for pelts, destabilized Indian settlement patterns along the Saginaw Bay. The Ottawa dominated, but were pushed out during the Iroquois Wars from 1641-1701.

After the defeat of the Iroquois in 1701, the French consolidated their fur-trading centers around a few select outposts. Fort Pontchartrain at Detroit was one of these posts built in 1701 by Antoine de la Mothe Cadillac. In order to develop the outpost, Cadillac invited tribes from the upper Great Lakes to settle in the vicinity of Fort Pontchartrain. Among these were Ojibwa who came down from northern Lake Huron. They gradually moved up from the north side of Lake St. Clair and scattered among the few remaining Ottawa along the Saginaw River.

As late as Pontiac's uprising in 1763, the region was characterized as being jointly occupied by Ottawa and Ojibwa. In fact, archaeological excavations at the Fletcher site, on the West Side of the river along Marquette Avenue, concluded in 1979 that a large clan of Ottawa and Ojibwa — numbering between 400 to 500 individuals — occupied this site between 1740 and 1765. After 1768, according to Helen H. Tanner, most of the Ottawa occupants joined other tribal members at L'Abre Croche (Cross Village) in the northwestern Lower Peninsula. After taking over Detroit from the French in 1760, the British began to use the term "Chippewa," a corruption of "Ojibwa," to refer to the Indian settlements along Saginaw Bay.

The cultural change produced by Indian contact with the white man was slow at first; however, as time passed the change became progressively more rapid until eventually there was little resemblance between what had been the Anishnabeg-Woodland tribes and what became the Ojibwa and Ottawa. The white man's arrival began the process of reducing the Indian to a mere cog in the economic machinery of an empire devouring fur-bearing animals. Economic exploitation would soon destroy completely that delicate balance between man and his environment that native cultures had already partially altered. When the United States took possession of the Great Lakes and settlers started moving north, the Ojibwa of the bay region began to experience final displacement.

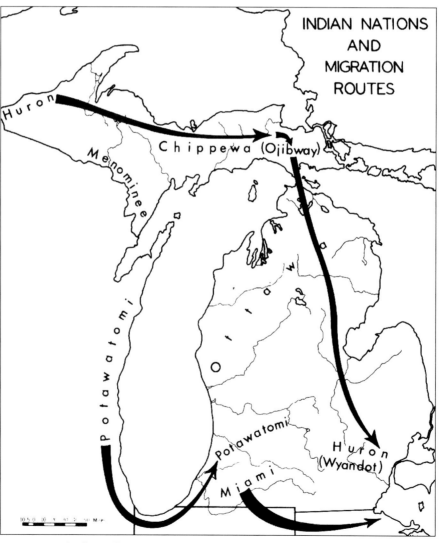

Indian tribes and patterns of settlement in Michigan.

Legend Check

THE ELUSIVE SAUK

For 150 years historians and archaeologists have accepted as fact that the Sauk Indians once roamed the Saginaw River region and their presence here was responsible for the derivation of the name "Saginaw." Innumerable references—history books, newspaper articles, and even archaeological journals, including the 1989 *Encyclopedia of Michigan,* continue to claim that "Saginaw" is derived from the Ottawa (not Ojibwa) term "Saug-e-nah," "O Saug-e-nong," or "Sag-a-nong," freely translated into "Land of the Sauks."

In 1966, Ottawa historian Francis Wakefield, writing in *Michigan History,* convincingly disclaimed the Sauk's presence in the valley, as well as the etymological derivation of the term "Saginaw." Wakefield wrote that Samuel de Champlain first met the Ottawa near Lake Nipissing in 1615, and was told that they were at war with the "Fire Nation," ten days journey west. A ten-day canoe journey would be approximately 600 miles. Champlain then recorded the "Fire Nation" or "Sauks" on his 1632 map as being located in the Lower Peninsula along the Saginaw Bay, a mere 130 miles west. Unfortunately, Champlain was unaware of the existence of Lake Michigan at the time. He assumed there was only one Great Lake and that the Ottawa's enemies were across it and on the south end of a large bay on Lake Huron. Champlain placed the Sauk in Michigan rather than in Wisconsin on the western shore of Lake Michigan where they actually lived. Here they were called the "Mascoutens," or "people of the prairies," not the incorrectly translated "fire people." French maps for centuries used Champlain's reference and soon Saginaw became the "Land of the Sauks." "Sak" or "Sag" is an Ottawa term actually meaning "to flow out" or "go outward." The prefix is widely used in its Indian derivation where a river flows out into a lake. Hence Saugatuck, MI., the Sagueney River in Quebec, or Sakinak where the Rock River flows into the Mississippi, and Segwun (Lowell), MI. Thus Ottawa references to "Sag-a-nah," meant "where the river flows out" and not "Land of the Sauks."

What all of this means of course, is that the Sauk were probably never present along the Saginaw River. Wakefield denies their presence, and Helen H. Tanner's recent and definitive *Atlas of Great Lakes Indian History* never places the Sauk anywhere near the Saginaw Bay except briefly when Cadillac invited some Wisconsin Sauk to Detroit in 1701. Archaeologists have found no evidence of permanent Sauk occupation in the valley and the Sauks themselves—outside of legend—never have claimed territorial rights in the Lower Peninsula. Still, Chippewa legend and some historians continue to claim the Saginaw region as the land of the Sauks. Archaeological evidence and Ottawa etymology suggest that it is time to stop repeating the myth that "Saginaw" is the "Land of the Sauks."

This drawing depicts a Sauk tribal war-dance prior to battle. It is doubtful that the Sauk ever lived in the Saginaw Valley.

Legend Check

THE BATTLE OF SKULL ISLAND?

Think about the implications! If the Sauk were never present along the Saginaw Bay, how could they have been massacred at the legendary battle of Skull Island by a grand alliance of Ojibwa, Ottawa, and Potawatomi? Are Indian legends any more correct or incorrect than folklore passed on by the white man? Does an oral history rather than a written one, in a culture without writing, guarantee a higher degree of accuracy?

According to the legend—often repeated by Natives and whites—the eastern Lower Peninsula was once inhabited by Sauk tribes. They concentrated their villages along the Saginaw River. Accounts of French missionaries and early explorers who had contact with the Sauk in Wisconsin, said they were a fierce, "savage" tribe constantly at war with neighboring bands. Indian oral history records that sometime in the mid-seventeenth century the people of the "three fires"—Ojibwa, Ottawa, and Potawatomi—united and attacked the Sauk along the Saginaw River. The battle culminated with a fierce struggle on Skull Island in Bay County. The Sauk were virtually all killed—hence the name Skull Island—and those few who survived were delivered as captives into Wisconsin. Subsequently, according to the myth, ghosts of the dead Sauk roamed the valley attacking and killing Ojibwa trappers and hunters. The Saginaw Valley became known as the "Forbidden Valley," and until the middle of the eighteenth century, few Indians dared trespass among the dead Sauk.

Some contemporary archaeologists and historians now doubt the reality of the popular legend. Chronicled perhaps first by William R. McCormick in 1835, it was also heard by Alexis de Tocqueville and Gustave de Beaumont on their visit to Saginaw in 1831, and has reappeared in every Bay City history since the mid-nineteenth century. It may be appropriate to reconsider the myth of the battle of Skull Island.

No archaeological evidence has been found to support the belief that there was ever any long-term Sauk occupation along the Saginaw. Skull Island itself has never been accurately located. McCormick claims it was an island once above what is now called Stone Island; Edgar M. Woods, writing in the *Bay City Times* in 1934, located it south of Brooks on the West Side and then part of the mainland; George Butterfield (1959) locates it south of there at the mouth of Squaconning Creek; and Leslie Arndt (1982) places it further south on the opposite shore and at the mouth of Cheboyganning Creek near Clements Airport. If indeed legendary skulls were once found there, they were probably remains of Indian smallpox victims and not remnants of a fierce battle. Lastly, during the French-fur trade era and Iroquois Wars the Saginaw Valley became relatively unimportant as the Natives gathered around posts at Detroit and Mackinac. It was not the ghosts of dead Sauk warriors that kept the Ojibwa from the Saginaw but simply warfare and economic disinterest.

Several events may explain the legend. A number of fierce battles between alliances of various Michigan tribes and their enemies took place in the seventeenth and eighteenth centuries. During the Iroquois Wars, Ojibwa, Ottawa, and Nipissing warriors defeated the Iroquois in 1662 at Pt. Iroquois, MI. (Bay Mills); in 1696, at the mouth of the Saugeen River, south of Georgian Bay, Ontario, Missisauga, Ottawa and Ojibwa, fought a climactic battle in which they overwhelmed the Iroquois and triumphantly ended the Iroquois Wars. The Missisauga, an Ojibwa-speaking peoples, subsequently occupied the Saginaw Valley. (The "Missisauga," sometimes called the "Saulteurs," could easily have been misidentified by the French as Sauks. E. F. Greenman, writing in the *Michigan History* believes that Nouvel visited the Missisauga, or "sakis," in Saginaw in 1675.) Finally, Ojibwa and Ottawa warriors annihilated the Sauk and Fox tribes at St. Croix Falls, Wisconsin in 1780.

These battles are what legends are made of, and while the Ojibwa-Ottawa may never have defeated their enemies along the Saginaw, their victories were legend even if their localities were sometime misplaced through oral tradition.

Henry Schoolcraft's early book on Indian tribes included this drawing of Great Lakes Indians striking the war post before going into battle.

William R. McCormick

ARCHAEOLOGY IN BAY COUNTY

Archaeology is a science that was lifted from pure treasure hunting. In time, people began to learn that a great deal of knowledge could be gleaned from some of the simplest artifacts representing the long-forgotten past. Bay City has not only had its share of archaeological discoveries, but also its share of treasure hunters. In 1967, when the Army Corps of Engineers was preparing to dredge the Saginaw River, a bulldozer uncovered a number of Indian burials at the old Fletcher Oil Company site. Word spread rapidly, and by that same afternoon, over 500 "treasure seekers" overran the property.

Fortunately, by the next day, the Fletcher site was brought under control and, despite the plunder, has proven to be one of the most valuable digs in the state for understanding Ojibwa customs. Over 75 sites are found in Bay County, and most of these are within a mile of the Saginaw Bay. Here are preserved remnants of villages, fishing camps, burials, and mounds. Some sites have been occupied by several different Native cultures often hundreds of years apart. One such site is the Fletcher dig now listed on the National Historic Register of Historic Places.

Not all archaeological digs involve prehistoric peoples. In any place where humans lived for a period of time, they inevitably left debris and thus a record of human history. The historic Trombley House was moved across the river in 1981. Its 150 year-old foundation, at 24th and Water streets, was excavated in 1982 and provided a wealth of new information about Bay City's pioneers and early settlement. [See Box Chapter 2] The Trombley House is also on the National Historic Register.

Archaeological methods employed at these recent site excavations have involved modern and sophisticated science. Today subsurface archaeology and the meticulous study of charcoals, firepits, burials, refuse pits, cisterns, and even outhouses provides much detailed information about prehistoric—before written records—and even historic life. Accidental or purposeful tampering with an historic site often leaves the experts at a disadvantage because the site becomes rearranged. The Bay County area has had its share of dedicated and conscientious amateur and professional archaeologists from Walter L. Schmidt in the 1920s, to George and Ira Butterfield, and Dr. Earl Prahl. Today's archaeologists do not necessarily give definitive answers about the nature of past cultures. They accept the challenge that they may be proven wrong,—as with the Moundbuilders—but their quest is to question and explore the past more deeply and to carry that knowledge one step further.

Local-site archaeology, 1982, Trombley House.

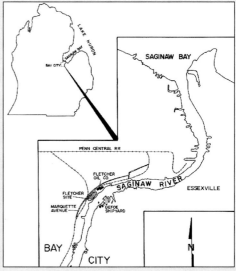
Location of the Fletcher site, 1970

INDIAN PLACE NAMES

Many of the landmark locations in and around Bay County continue to be called by the descriptive place names used by the area's Native Americans to identify gathering spots, fishing sites, or hunting grounds:

Tobico: Ojibwa, Pe-to-be-goong, "the little lake by the big lake."
Kawkawlin: Ojibwa, Uh-guh-konning, "the place of the pickerel."
Tittabawassee: Ojibwa, Ta-te-bwa-saik, "the water that runs slowly," or "the water that runs parallel to the shore."
Pineconning: Ojibwa, Pinne-koning, "the place of the little potatoes."
Quanicassee: Ojibwa, Poh-gwon-ke-zee, "the place of the lone tree."
Nayanquing: Ojibwa, Nayah-quong, "end of the woods."
Wenonah: The mother of "Hiawatha" in Longfellow's poem by that name.
Saginaw: Ottawa, O-sauge-e-nong, "to flow out of," or "where the river flows out."
Squaconning Creek: Ojibwa, Es-qua-kon-ing, "the last creek," last tributary on Saginaw prior to joining the bay.
Cheboyganing Creek: Ojibwa, Pub-wuh-guh-ning, "place of the wild rice."
Sebewaing: Ojibwa, Sobe-wens, "little river."

CHAPTER 2: "LOWER SAGINAW"

The early pioneers came into the valley too soon to get rich. They only opened the way for those who came after them to make their fortunes.
William R. McCormick, *The Saginawian*, 1874

THE OJIBWA AND THE FUR TRADE

Native Americans played a diminishing historical role as the frontier gave way to settlement along the Saginaw Bay shore. The fur trade had been leaving lower Michigan since 1800, shifting to Canada and westward. This trade established the Ojibwa as the dominant tribe in the Saginaw area in the latter half of the eighteenth and early nineteenth centuries. These peoples lived primarily by fishing and hunting/gathering, and as a result they controlled key village sites around the bay and along the Saginaw River. From these locations they harvested the beaver and traded first with the French and later the British. Neither nation established permanent trading posts along Saginaw Bay. Ojibwa fur-trade activity took place here only after the American occupation occurred in the early nineteenth century, but by then the golden days of the trade were quickly passing.

Shortly before the War of 1812 and after the United States gained control of the Great Lakes, John Jacob Astor organized the American Fur Company. This new venture was a combination of the Old Northwest Company and the British owned Mackinaw Company that he had bought out. At the end of the war, Astor located trading posts at strategic sites along the Great Lakes' shores. In 1816, Louis Campau, working for the American Fur Company, built a log trading post in present day Saginaw. Prior to Campau's outpost, several rough-hewn cabins were built along the bay and near the mouth of the river. Louis and Gassette Trombley may have located here for a short period of time prior to Campau. Louis was apparently lost when his sloop disappeared in Saginaw Bay in 1792. Jacob Graveradt, a Dutch trader, and Stephen V. Riley, the son of an Ojibwa woman and Dutch trader, also were known to have lived here shortly after the war.

Dependence on furs made the Ojibwa laborers for the white traders, but it also gave them access to new technology. Furs, used to make fashionable beaver hats in France, were exchanged for guns, knives, hatchets, blankets, clothing, flour, corn, and other manufactured items. Gradually the white man's tools began to make dramatic changes in Ojibwa culture. Their use of trade

Above: Shoppenogons and his family outside of their cabin, c. 1880s.
Left: Chief Shoppenogons posed for this studio photograph in the late nineteenth century. Shoppenogons traveled frequently between Bay City and Grayling and was well-known and respected as a representative of the Ojibwa people. He died in 1911.

goods lessened their reliance on farming and fishing. As their livelihood changed the Ojibwa also saw the natural world around them change.

Firearms, for example, had a direct and immediate effect. Relying on the musket, the Ojibwa began to depend almost exclusively on game-animals for food. Increased hunting quickly depleted big game like elk and moose. Traditional sanctions that had guided the Indians' relationships with the land diminished as new economic influences and technologies altered patterns of life. Harvesting furs encouraged wholesale slaughter of the beaver and brought the population near extinction by 1820. Large beaver populations had regulated river ecology, but the drastic drop in the number of animals further changed the nature of Saginaw Bay. Wanton destruction of beaver ponds lowered interior water levels and brought runoff and silt quickly into the bay. Fewer fish species then sought the bay's murky spawning grounds.

As the fur trade was coming to an end, the Indians became less involved in the destruction of forest resources for the whites. However, they became even more dependent on the white man for food and staples. Their traditional trapping skills no longer important to white settlers, the Ojibwa became insulated in villages along Saginaw Bay. Again they attempted to subsist by employing old fishing and farming practices. At times they worked sporadically for the whites, but in most instances they resisted assimilation by maintaining their culture and language in isolated settlements or churches like the Kawkawlin Indian church. [See Box] Still they needed trade goods, and with little left to trade they sold their last possession—their land.

INDIAN TREATIES

During the War of 1812, the Ojibwa abandoned trade with the American Fur Company and quickly gave support to the British against the Americans. The Indians did not see English settlers as land-grabbers. When the war was over, the British gave guarantees not to stir up Native resistance against the Americans; however, the English remained visibly present on the lakes. Lewis Cass, Governor of the Michigan Territory and Superintendent of Indian Affairs in the Northwest, reported from Detroit that the Ojibwa were hostile and kept the area in a state of "feverish alarm." Cass was fearful of a renewed Native alliance, like Tecumseh's in 1812, being revived by the British.

Lewis Cass, Territorial Governor of Michigan, 1813-1831.

THE INDIAN MISSION CHURCH AT KAWKAWLIN

As the fur trade began to decline in the Saginaw Bay area around 1830, nearby Ojibwa, having lost their livelihood and their land, became increasingly insulated in villages along rivers of the bay. They survived here by returning to subsistence patterns of hunting-fishing-gathering and occasionally working for nearby townspeople. Apprehensive of their future, they resisted assimilation into the white man's world by maintaining their language and cultural activities in clan-like settlements.

One such settlement sprang up around the first church built in Bay County. The Methodist Indian Mission Church in Kawkawlin was built by a Rev. Brown in 1847. The original building, which still stands, was constructed about midway between the village of Kawkawlin and the river. Today it is located at the intersection of Hidden Rd. and North Euclid. In 1883, the community consisted of about 40 families and a Rev. Cloud acted as pastor. Today only about 20 Indians remain.

Efforts have been made to preserve the structure and it was renovated in 1986. Because so much of the Ojibwa's way of life was tied to the environment, the elders for over a century have tried to preserve—in the face of environmental change—simple lifestyles and beliefs before they completely disappear. Much of this spirit is captured in the Kawkawlin Mission Church, and many Ojibwa still see it as a source that preserves their past.

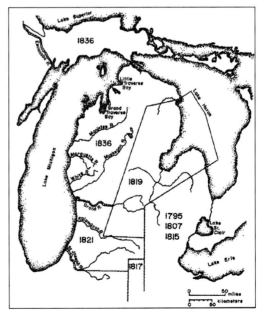

In the Treaty of Saginaw, 1819, the Saginaw Ojibwa sold for $3,000, plus $1,000 annually "forever," six million acres of land and parts of Lake Huron, outlined above, to the United States.

Captain Joseph F. Marsac was an interpreter and advisor to Gov. Cass during the 1819 Saginaw Treaty negotiations. He later returned to Portsmouth and lived in a house on Harrison Street.

Even after the War of 1812, the British continued to engage in the fur trade and stir up the Indians on Lake Huron from this post on St. Joseph Island in the North Channel.

In order to counter British influence among the Indians, Cass negotiated the 1819 Treaty of Saginaw and built Fort Saginaw in 1822. Although past interpretations of the 1819 treaty emphasize the interests of land speculators in spurring negotiations with the Indians, it now appears Cass was more concerned with securing control of the Great Lakes and eliminating the influence of the British fur traders. Astor's fur company, with its strategic outposts in place, was the tool Cass used to drive British traders and their Indian allies out of the territory. Fort Saginaw was but one of a dozen military posts the Governor built for the purpose of closing lines of commerce between the British and the Ojibwa.

In September, 1819, along the west bank of the river in old Saginaw City where Louis Campau had built a spacious, open-air council house, Cass met with the Indians. The Ojibwa were reluctant participants in the treaty negotiations. Chief O-ge-ma Ke-ga-to told Cass they had only come to smoke the pipe of peace following the war, and that they had no intention of selling Indian lands. Cass reminded the Natives, that as allies with the recently vanquished British, the Ojibwa had little claim to lost lands, and that they could be asked to leave the territory and move west. During the 10 to 12 days of the council, Cass eventually went around the chiefs and bribed trusted traders—Steven Riley and Jacob Smith—with land grants. They in turn were able to convince the Ojibwa leaders, who were also granted large reservations, to agree to terms. The chiefs also received $3,000 and agreed to sign to avoid the fate of relocation westward.

The treaty established one large, 40,000-acre, reservation on the West Side of Bay City, and a smaller one for John Riley, Steven's son, on the East Side near what is now the downtown business section. Cass also promised a blacksmith to keep Ojibwa muskets in good repair and an agricultural teacher. These provisions were fulfilled, but the blacksmith was located in Lower Saginaw (Bay City) far from Indian settlements. The agricultural teacher was sent to Saginaw in order to speed up the process of civilizing

The placement of a memorial stone in Roosevelt Park for O-ge-ma Ke-ga-to who spoke for the Ojibwa at the 1819 treaty. Chief Ogemaw's remains were moved to this historic Native gathering place in 1923.

the Natives and removing them from participating in the British fur trade.

Although Cass did build a military outpost in Saginaw in 1822, malaria and typhoid incapacitated the garrison. It was recalled to Detroit in 1823. The fort was abandoned, and except for a few traders, the blacksmith, and a handful of Ojibwa, the Saginaw River and Bay receded into the wilderness.

Settlements at "Lower Saginaw"

On July 27, 1831, the wilderness around what was to become Bay City, had two famous visitors. Alexis de Tocqueville, author of *Democracy in America,* and his traveling companion Gustave de Beaumont were two young, French aristocrats traveling to America to observe Native Americans and the wilderness. Both Tocqueville, in a *Fortnight in the Wilderness,* and Beaumont, in his novel *Marie,* would recapture in detail their overland trek from Detroit to Saginaw. They came at a time when the Saginaw Bay area was about to change from a wilderness outpost to an area of "flourishing cities."

On that steamy day in July, 1831, the two Frenchmen intended to leave Saginaw and once again "penetrate the humid depths for Detroit." However, their horses still had saddle sores from their ride two days earlier from Detroit, and this persuaded them to stay another day. To pass the time, Tocqueville and Beaumont descended the Saginaw toward its mouth to hunt. In doing so they passed through the vast prairies that would some day be Bay City. Tall grass, snakes, and mosquitoes are what impressed them the most. The prairies were separated from Saginaw City by miles of intermittent swamps. These same swamps isolated Bay City from Saginaw for decades and encouraged individuality and town rivalries that persist to this day.

Alexis de Tocqueville

Joseph Trombley

Mader Trombley

Had Tocqueville and Beaumont trekked nearer the mouth of the Saginaw, they undoubtedly would have met Leon Trombley—one of a score of Trombleys about to settle Bay City—building his log cabin along the east side of the river near present-day downtown. Trombley came from Detroit in 1831 as a government agricultural agent to teach the Indians to farm. He also came to cultivate the fur trade as well as potatoes. Trombley cleared half an acre of fertile ground on the prairie, planted a crop for the Indians and himself, built a one-room log cabin, and then returned to Detroit to get his family.

Though Trombley returned, he did not remain long along the "lower Saginaw." Even an offer by the Indians to swap one section (360 acres) of reservation land along the river for his horse could not persuade Trombley to stay. Later he recalled: "Who would have thought a city would one day stand where there was nothing but swamp, with long grass—where there was scarcely an opening in the woods, and in which the wolves made plenty of howling." Tocqueville would later write about the dishonest traders he met along the Saginaw. Apparently Trombley was either honest enough not to dupe the Indians of their land, considered the land worthless (which was most likely), or was so unsure of Indian title that he made no effort to engage in land speculation.

Few settlers trickled into the lower Saginaw area before Michigan became a state in 1837. Louis Masho, a French trader lived for awhile with his Indian wife near the river at Lafayette Street. In 1834 Benjamin Cushway, a trader and government agent like Trombley, built a log cabin and a blacksmith's shop on the west bank near the old 23rd Street bridge. Also in 1834 John B. Trudell, another fur trader turned fisherman, built a third log cabin just south of Trombley's. Around this time,

Left: The Center House, or old McCormick residence built on corner of 24th and Water streets, is thought to be the oldest standing frame house in Bay City. It was moved to the Veterans Park area in 1981.
Right: Bay City, 1838. Globe Hotel is in center, to the right is the wildcat bank building, storehouse, and small log house. All were near present-day Fourth and Water streets.

R. Elliot's Blacksmith Shop, in West Bay City.

Joseph and Mader Trombley, nephews of Leon, also moved into the area. Joseph built a cabin and heavily stocked it for Indian trade in 1832 or 1833 at Portsmouth in south Bay City.

The Trombley brothers are considered Bay City's first real settlers because they came with a definite idea of developing the region. They purchased a 312-acre tract along the river, about three miles south of Leon's cabin, and in doing so in 1834, secured the first government land patent in the area. The Trombleys also brought cattle with them and later—now believed to have been around 1839—constructed a large frame house on high ground near the river in Portsmouth. The Center or Trombley House was to be used as a trading post and residence, but recent archaeological studies indicate that it was more a center for land speculation than an outpost for the fur trade. [See box page 27]

The Trombleys, Cushway, and Trudell were soon followed by the promoters. Albert Miller, recently appointed judge of probate in Saginaw County (1835), purchased land from the Trombleys in 1836. In July, he hired a surveyor and laid out the town of Portsmouth. Miller's Portsmouth Company was responsible for the first "paper city" in Bay County. The town extended north and south about 13 blocks from Columbus Avenue to 32nd Street. The town's streets were laid out in a basic grid pattern that ran from the river eight blocks east to South Jefferson. Miller left for Detroit and tried to sell lots, but apparently finding little interest, he sold parts of his city to Governor Stevens T. Mason and Henry Schoolcraft, noted Indian Agent for Michigan. Refinanced, Miller returned to Portsmouth, built a sawmill and drew a new plat map for the city. Lots were soon being promoted in Detroit and Saginaw City; however before any settlers arrived the Panic of 1837 struck. The sawmill at Portsmouth was closed and Miller retired to a farm near Saginaw.

Additional treaties with the Indians in 1837 extinguished most Ojibwa land claims to the territory around Bay City. The Riley reserve, where downtown Bay City now stands, was sold to the Saginaw Bay Land Company in 1836. This land company was owned by James Fraser, a recent Scottish immigrant, who attracted several investors, including again Governor Mason. Fraser surveyed the land and laid out the paper village of "Lower Saginaw" in 1837, just as Miller was building his sawmill in Portsmouth. The new town's streets paralleled the river—they were not true north and south as in nearby Portsmouth—for fourteen blocks and eastward into the interior about ten blocks. The Saginaw Bay Company built several structures in 1837-38 to stimulate land sales. A warehouse, a large dock, a square log blockhouse, and a small bank building were erect-

Judge Albert Miller

James Fraser

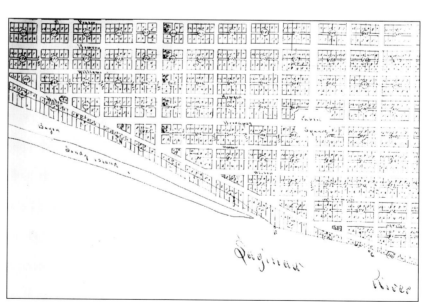

Portsmouth in 1856. The new town's streets, laid out in 1836, ran north and south, and it was the first "paper city" in Bay County.

Governor Stevens T. Mason

James G. Birney

Legend Check

THE CENTER HOUSE

Rock-solid beliefs once part of the historical foundation of Bay City have been dug up and cast aside by archaeologists working at the site of the historic Trombley House.

The Trombley House—or Center House—has long been regarded as Bay City's oldest frame building. Reportedly built in 1837 in Portsmouth at the corner of Twenty-fourth and Water Streets by Joseph and Mader Trombley, it was to serve as a fur-trade outpost, store, and residence. In 1979, the Bay County Historical Society accepted the challenge of restoring the building. With a good deal of private and community support, the structure was lifted from its century-old foundation, placed on a river barge, and floated to a new location across the Saginaw River in 1981. A year later archaeologist, Dr. Earl J. Prahl, organized a team of professionals and volunteers to undertake extensive examination of the foundation.

Archaeological evidence revealed several new interpretations about the house and early Bay City. The most popular historic idea of the Center House as a trading post was not supported by the evidence gathered. Prahl concludes that the building probably was foremost an inn or boardinghouse in its early days. Little in the way of fur-trade goods or beaver remains were found. Moreover, a great deal of inexpensive ceramic and glass dishware confirm that the building was probably used as a boardinghouse. While removing the old siding from the building, the word "Centre" (French *au Centre*) was found painted in large letters on the north side confirming its probable use as a gathering place.

The date of construction also has been pushed forward to between 1839 and 1842. Economic conditions in 1837, building materials used, and historic observations do not support the often-cited year of 1837 as the construction date.

Lastly, the complete array of evidence seems to indicate that early occupants of the Trombley House were engaged in a variety of lifestyles. They were not fur traders, but land speculators, fishermen, and farmers. They may have been unscrupulous in their dealings with the Indians—as James Birney and de Tocqueville described; and, as archaeologist Prahl concludes, maybe they were "a little too quick to grasp the chance to prosper." We should not, as the archaeologists tell us, necessarily accept them as founders and heroes of our early city. They were pioneer settlers struggling to make a living in a rapidly changing frontier environment.

The Trombley or Center House, c. 1930.

The Center House enroute to Veterans Park by barge, 1981.

ed. It also appears that the Globe Hotel was built around this time in Lower Saginaw. The hurried construction was completed just in time to suffer the effects of the 1837 Panic. With few lots sold, Fraser temporarily abandoned the scheme. The blockhouse was burned and the bank closed. A smallpox epidemic in 1837, especially among the Ojibwa, disrupted public health and further discouraged settlement.

Disastrous economic conditions continued into the 1840s, and little activity took place around either Lower Saginaw or Portsmouth for five years. In 1843, Fraser restructured the Saginaw Bay Land Company with the financial aid of James G. Birney and his brother-in-law, Daniel H. Fitzhugh. Birney, who ran for the presidency as an anti-slavery candidate in 1844 while a resident of Bay City, directed changes in Lower Saginaw's town plan. He now included two parks, and in every other block set aside two lots for churches. Religious groups would become owners of the land upon construction of a church on the lot. Birney moved to Lower Saginaw in 1842 and plunged into farming both sides of the river. He sold off an inherited southern plantation and now had sufficient capital to own and manage the development of Lower Saginaw as a resident promoter. Fitzhugh remained in New York to sell lots and attract settlers to the river settlement.

Birney's entrepreneurial-promotional interests conflicted with his moral values and may explain why Bay City never developed as quickly as Saginaw City or East Saginaw. From Lower Saginaw Birney often wrote to Fitzhugh deploring the treatment of the Indians. He noted that he had frequently to "raise his voice against the inequity of making the Indians drunk and cheating them." His outbursts brought resentment from traders and slowed settlement. He also insisted on regular religious services. All of this moral uplift was probably out of place in a frontier town based on land speculation.

Birney worked hard to secure a post office at Lower Saginaw (1846); built the first school; and in 1847 constructed a sawmill. Yet by mid-century, Lower Saginaw and Portsmouth still were villages of a few log houses, shanties along the river, and small farms all hemmed in by mosquito-infested swamps and forests. There were no streets and the mud and water along the pathways was ankle deep. The population, according to Birney, numbered only 130 residents. After 15 years of effort, town promotion—often dominated by outside investors from Detroit and New York—failed along the lower Saginaw.

At mid-century, though, prospects for settlement began to improve. In the winter of 1847, wealthy lumberman Henry Sage came from New York to buy timber for his yards in Ithaca. Sage and several companions took a sleigh downriver with the intention of purchasing land in Lower Saginaw from Birney. However, Birney was too ill to even meet with visitors and they

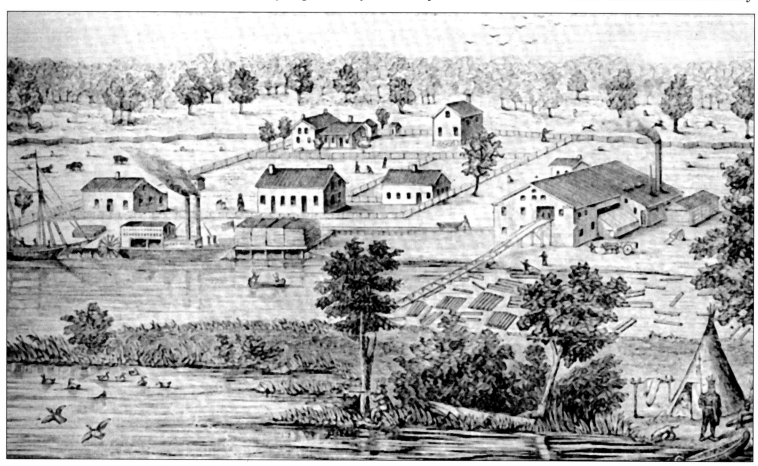

Lower Saginaw in 1854. There were already about 12 sawmills along the river in Bay City and still several hundred Natives dwelling in the area.

returned the next day without negotiating the sale.

Birney's ill health and his apparent ability to discourage settlers prompted Fitzhugh to send his son, Daniel, Jr., to Lower Saginaw. He brought more money with him and tried to infuse new life into the barren village. Fitzhugh constructed a new sawmill and used the wood to build "a very pretentious dwelling along the river." In 1851, however, the sawmill was blown up killing the fireman and destroying the mill's machinery. Fitzhugh, Jr. returned East that year to attend to his father's real estate business.

Fitzhugh's misfortune did not dissuade others from seeing the potential in tapping the area's timber resources. Between 1850 and 1854, 12 new sawmills were built in Lower Saginaw. Though they were small and crudely equipped, the new mills brought workers and small-scale development. A doctor and a lawyer arrived, the Fraser House and Wolverton House hotels were built, and several boardinghouses were constructed near the sawmills. In 1857, Bay County was organized and separated from Saginaw and Midland counties despite the opposition from Saginaw merchants and politicians. When the state legislature finally approved the county measure, its legality was challenged all the way to the Michigan Supreme Court where the act was upheld in 1858. The political and legal obstructionism that Saginaw used to block Bay County's beginnings generated ill feelings between the two cities that persisted for decades. At the same time county status was granted, Birney renamed the settlement "Bay City."

In 1859, the village of Bay City incorporated with a population of 700. There were 14 sawmills in and near the city as the dawn of the lumber era was about to break. Fishing was an important export industry as it supplied settlers all along the Saginaw. Little effort at agriculture was made and residents continued to import foodstuffs from Saginaw farms. Transport was almost entirely by water, and there were no improved roads coming into the city. While the original town plat of Lower Saginaw was expanded south nearly to Portsmouth, there was little growth east into the forests away from the river. In 1860 the population of 810 people was scattered along nearly two miles of waterfront characterized by floating fishing barges, drying nets, twisted docks, sawmills, millponds, drying lumber, several boardinghouses, 12 saloons, and scattered business and homes. As one observer noted, "The physical beauty of the place was little improved."

The Globe Hotel is now thought to predate the Center House as the area's first frame structure and inn. It was built in 1838 by James Fraser's Saginaw Bay Company to promote settlement of Lower Saginaw.

James Fraser, one of the founders of Lower Saginaw, erected the Fraser House in 1865 at a cost of $75,000. It stood at the corner of Center and Water Streets and burned down in 1906. The site was occupied by the Wenonah Hotel until it burned in 1977 and now is where Delta College's Planetarium is located.

THE WEST SIDE

Across the river from Bay City and Portsmouth businessmen and ethnic settlers built three hamlets that would eventually become West Bay City. The oldest West Side settlement was the village of Banks. The Trombleys sold the Center House to William R. McCormick in 1845, and Joseph subsequently moved down river about two miles and settled in what was to become Banks. This village, built on low ground on the bend near the mouth of the Saginaw River, was settled by French fishermen. It was here that a flourishing yet very transient French community developed and maintained its identity into modern times. Trombley—now a fisherman and land speculator—platted out Banks into a 300 square-acre grid; but like Lower Saginaw, there was little growth until the late 1850s. By the end of the Civil War, three sawmills, several salt blocks, and fishing occupied the 400 residents.

Salt extracted from brine water beneath the cities of the Saginaw Valley became the economic reason for the founding of Salzburg. Scattered salt springs along the Saginaw had been known to Indians, and state geologists developed an interest in tapping this resource. In 1859, through efforts of several Saginaw lumbermen, the state legislature passed a bill granting a bounty of ten cents a bushel on manufactured salt and a tax exemption for property used in salt production. Sawmills producing salt as a by-product experienced a financial windfall. The bounty and tax exemption prompted Daniel Fitzhugh, Sr., who had recently moved to Bay City, and James Fraser to plat another speculative tract of land across the river from Portsmouth. A small, triangular town site was laid out and soon three salt-manufacturing establishments were built. Fitzhugh named the town site after the Austrian resort and salt-mining city of Salzburg. Although the salt bounty was repealed in 1862, all lots in the village were sold and five sawmills and salt works employed several hundred workers. Because of its location near the German settlement of Frankenlust, many German farmers migrated toward the sawmills, and soon Salzburg was a thoroughly German village.

After his trip to Saginaw in 1847, Henry Sage began to purchase thousands of acres of pinelands in northern Michigan. In 1860, his eastern pine depleted, Sage decided to move his sawmill operations west. Sage returned to Bay City and again tried to buy the site directly opposite Bay City from Birney's widow and Fitzhugh. They remained unwilling to sell, but Sage persistently returned three years in a row trying to negotiate a deal. Finally in 1863, a purchase price of $12,000 for 116 acres was agreed upon.

Sage purchased the land in partnership with John McGraw of Poughkeepsie, New York. By the spring of 1864, construction began on a sawmill. When the mill was placed in operation a year later, it was reported to be the largest sawmill in the world. Besides the sawmill, Sage opened a company store, a warehouse, a brick office building, a boardinghouse, a tenement apartment, and 20 individual dwellings. All of this was centered around today's Veterans Park—which was Sage's millpond—and called Wenona. A well-planned and controlled company town, Wenona grew rapidly. Sage poured nearly one million in expenditures into the settlement and attracted entrepreneurs and workers. Within two years there were 700 residents in the village. In 1877, the three West Side settlements united into West Bay City. Both Bay City (Portsmouth and Lower Saginaw) and West Bay City (Banks, Salzburg, and Wenona) were started as paper cities and speculative villages. However because they were established years apart and Wenona was a company town, there was little cross-river entrepreneurial rivalry as in Saginaw City and East Saginaw. The Trombleys, Fraser, Birney, and Fitzhugh were more conservative investors who struggled through difficult financial times and mixed entrepreneurial and moral ambitions to effect slow economic development. They hesitated to build a city and make internal improvements in advance of the lumber era. As the lumber era arrived, large investor-industrialists like Sage and McGraw moved into Bay City. These lumbermen built towns and established the economic framework for Bay City, but as absentee owners they never developed an interest in their community that would transcend their desire for profit. Absentee investment established a pattern that was to plague Bay City throughout its existence. Lastly with the settlement of French-speaking Banks and German-speaking Salzburg, a crazy-quilt pattern of ethnic enclaves also began to color Bay City's residential neighborhoods.

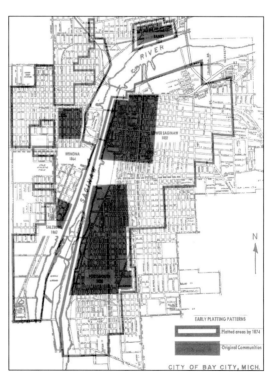

The location and names of the communities that eventually became Bay City in 1865.

TOLL ROADS IN BAY COUNTY

Early on Sunday morning the toll-gate keeper on the Vassar [Tuscola] plank, kept by Mrs. Hegle and her daughter Ada, was invaded by three men en masque.

One of them presented the muzzle of a revolver at the lady while the others ransacked the house, gobbling up $75 or $100 in currency.

Bay City Observer, February 8, 1877

By the time Mrs. Hegle and her daughter were so rudely awakened in 1877, Bay City's plank toll roads were about to be replaced. The lumber business and much of the commerce in early Bay City, before these roads were first built in 1860, was along the waterways. Bay County was a veritable swamp at its inception and as such it was almost impossible to build reliable, long-lasting roads. The lack of contact between Saginaw and Bay City, and subsequent city rivalries, originated in part because of the difficulty in getting from one town to the other. Sometimes it would take days for the small passenger boat to set off from Bay City to Saginaw. In 1860 the first road was built connecting the two cities along the old East Side Indian trail.

While there were a few dirt roads built earlier on high ground from Bay City, it was not until 1859 that the Tuscola Plank Road—the first improved road—was built south from Center Avenue to Blumfield Junction. It was apparently along this roadway that Mrs. Hegle was robbed. There were two toll gates along the Tuscola Road. One at Tuscola and Trumbull, and a second at Cass Avenue. Travelers had to pay a toll for use of the road depending on the number of horses, the size of the wagon, number of passengers, or miles traveled. In 1864, there were three stage lines to Saginaw operating along the road.

West Bay City received a $20,000 loan from the state to build the Midland Plank Road connecting it to the city of Midland in 1865. It took two days to travel back and forth between Midland and Bay City. There was a toll gate just outside of West Bay City and another in Auburn. The cost was about a dollar both ways depending on the number of passengers. Also in 1865 the U. S. Government, in order to facilitate state construction of roads through swamps, helped finance the Unionville Plank Road with a land grant. There were several other plank roads built in the next decade—one was Bullock Road in south Bay City, and another connected Banks, Wenona and later Kawkawlin in 1875.

While a number of experiments were made, including setting planks in tar and sawdust in Bay County, most construction followed traditional methods brought from Canada. Two parallel rows of timber were laid along the roadbed three feet apart. Planks eight to ten feet long and three or four inches thick were placed across the parallel "sleepers." These roads never lasted long in Bay County. Freezing, spring rains, swamps and soggy land warped and decayed the boards quickly. Many needed constant repair work, but since the county allowed citizens to "work out" their road tax, a good many repairs were simply "forgotten." By the 1880s the county began to build stone and macadam roads.

Workers lay cedar paving blocks along Bay City streets, c. 1870.

Midland Road ran from West Bay City to Midland in 1865. It was originally a dirt toll road and cost $1.00 to travel between cities.

BANKS AND "FRENCHTOWN"

The earliest European settlers in and around Bay City were primarily Frenchmen, or French-speaking Canadians, engaged in the fur trade and later in fishing, and lumbering. Following the Trombleys promotional efforts at Banks, many Frenchmen settled in that area on the west side of the Saginaw River's mouth and in Dolsenville—the area north of Woodside Avenue—also called "Frenchtown." By the 1880s almost 90 percent of the population living along both shores of the river at its mouth were French-speaking. St. Joseph's Church in Bay City was made up of French-speaking Catholics.

While the French did well as traders and fishermen, their populations burgeoned during the lumber era. Aggressively recruited by lumbermen to work in the woods, the French shanty boy, wood chopper, or "riverhog" was often seen in a class by himself. Many moved from Quebec and Ontario when the Canadian government refused to open vast interior lands to logging in the 1860s. Eventually, especially in the summer months, thousands moved into the cities to work in the sawmills. Though familiar with the primitive lumbering machinery from Canada, most Frenchmen viewed lumbering and logging as out-of-doors work. They did not adjust quickly to life in the sawmills.

Many Canadians were also recruited by absentee lumbermen and used as scab laborers in the sawmills during strikes. Though seen by the mill owners as "industrious, and docile" workers, as strikebreakers they often were not welcomed into the Bay City community. Given a choice, the French lumber worker would prefer riding logs down the river, and as a result they were the most transient of Bay City's ethnic groups. When the fall approached, the French Canadian quickly packed his "turkey" and headed into the woods. Bay City's river-side French population remained predominantly male, young, and transient. Nonetheless, they managed to establish ethnic enclaves in Banks and Frenchtown where the French culture persisted through the mid-twentieth century.

Left: French fishermen in the Banks area.

Below: Beebe Fishworks at the mouth of Saginaw River in 1870s.

GERMANS AT FRANKENLUST

The German settlement at Frankenlust—centered around St. Paul's Lutheran Church on M-84—began as a spin-off congregation from the original "Franconian" community in Frankenmuth. In April, 1845, Pastor August Craemer arrived in south Saginaw County with a hearty band of German Lutherans from Neuendettelsau. The original purpose of the movement according to legend and Lutheran tradition was to provide religious instruction to the Indians. However, most came as one contemporary noted, because "of famine or the threat of hunger and the one great cause was the desire for political and religious freedom."

Recent examination of census data reveals that many German communities moved enmasse from Germany to Michigan. Common religions, villages, and even neighborhoods often bound immigrants together. This provincial commonality, especially in rural areas, sustained long periods of ethnic-religious identity.

Such was the case in 1847 when a second colony of settlers came and was directed to settle in Frankenlust. Pastor Ferdinand Sievers gathered the Germans together along the headwaters of Squaconning Creek. Today this river has been dredged and for most of its length is a county drain; but in 1851 it was described as "a small river, wide and deep enough for navigation of steamers and sail boats. In November, 1849, a steamer, 120 feet long, docked in front of the Church [at Frankenlust] and unloaded provisions."

A year earlier, Pastor Sievers "rejoiced in the dedication of their new house of worship at Frankenlust hewn logs and 28 feet in length and 24 feet wide."

Sievers remained pastor until 1893—46 years. Frankenlust was a community that for decades clung to its German language and customs and established parochial schools to maintain that culture. In 1905 the present church was built on the site of the first log church. Frankenlust became a long-term success and served as the beginning for such churches as Immanuel Lutheran (1861), St, John's in Amelith (1852), and Zion Lutheran (1901). The prosperity at Frankenlust also encouraged the process of "chain migration" where one immigrant family would write a "letter from America" and encourage others to follow the trans-Atlantic chain of emigrants to the New World. Some also came as single farm laborers and worked for Frederick Koch at Amelith. Koch, Rev. Siever's father-in-law, built a "blockhouse" dormitory here in 1850 and contracted out German immigrants as "serfs" to nearby farmers. A good many of these men later found work in the sawmills and salt industries of Salzburg.

Pastor Ferdinand Sievers led the Frankenlust settlers to Squaconning Creek in 1847.

St. Paul's Lutheran Church on M-84 at I-75. Outside of the Indian mission church in Kawkawlin, this is the oldest congregation in Bay County. Pictured here is the second structure built in 1905.

The original Michigan Haus restaurant on M-84 was a part of the Frakenlust settlement.

CHAPTER 3: LUMBERTOWN ENTERPRISES

> *The lumber tract comprised in the Saginaw Valley is probably the most extensive as well as the most valuable in the world. The quantity of timber is so great that it must afford an abundant supply for generations to come.*
>
> *Saginaw Valley Pioneer Directory*, 1866

LOGGING

Although the above optimistic statement of abundance was to apply to only one generation, it characterized the unbridled optimism of early Bay City. By the 1870s lumbering employed more workers than any other industrial occupation in the United States, and the center of logging and lumbering for the nation was the Saginaw Valley. It is one of those grand epochs that historical amnesia has allowed to fade in perspective. The mansions on Center Avenue are about all that remains to remind residents of the once proud lore of logs and lumber. Cutting logs into lumber is what established Bay City, set the stage for entrepreneurial growth, brought in diverse populations, and made the community what it became one hundred years later. In short, lumbering is Bay City's legacy.

The pine tree was the "green gold" that attracted lumbermen to Michigan. Pine forest covered about two-thirds of the Lower Peninsula. The tallest and clearest pine was located north of the frost-free line from Bay City to Muskegon. Here were often found belts of pine trees—like the one running for 80 miles in Gladwin County along the Tittabawassee River—that were often considered some of the best pine in the eastern U. S. Full-grown trees often reached 175 feet in height and 2 to 7 feet in diameter.

Though the presence of pine was crucial, the location of Bay City is what actually made it prosper. At the mouth of the Saginaw River, Bay City's sawmills could be fed by a tributary system of rivers and streams that ran 900 miles into the interior forests. These waterways were to become the main arteries by which logs could be moved cheaply to the

Photographs like this one were common by the 1870s. Traveling photographers visited the interior sawmill camps, took photographs, and sold each one for a dollar. Weeks later developed photos were mailed back to each shanty boy who had purchased one. Note the pride the teamsters have showing their horses.

sawmills. Bay City's access to the bay and Great Lakes offered inexpensive transportation to major markets. Without these rivers the timber would have remained inaccessible. It was almost natural that eastern investors would build their sawmill towns at the mouth of the Saginaw.

The lumbermen-entrepreneurs who built the mills or company towns came with a single purpose—to make money. They were not early town-builders or moralists like James Birney. And because of the insatiable demand for finished lumber, an endless supply of timber, and undisciplined markets, lumbermen sought immediate, short term profits often at the expense of the community and the workers. In short they set an exploitative pattern Bruce Catton explained well: "Take what there is, take all of it, and take it as fast as you can, and let tomorrow's people handle tomorrow's problems."

Early investors picked townsites at the mouths of rivers. Water transportation was the cheapest and quickest way to move goods before the advent of the railroad in the 1840s in Michigan.

This winter camp photograph depicts the shanty boys with horse and oxen teams. A temporary railroad bed has been laid to move logs to a nearby river banking grounds. Look at the men and notice how comfortable they are with their draft animals.

Camp Life

A typical dining hall in a northern Michigan logging camp. This is probably a camp in the 1870s. Three and four meals a day were served. The men generally ate well and "tied on" to a particular camp often because of the cook's reputation.

This scene depicts the generally well-paid cook staff and a young man holding the "gabriel" or "gaberal," a tin horn used to call the shanty boys in for meals. It was also called a "gut horn." This is taken at Jonathan Boyce's camp, 1893, Houghton Lake, MI.

"Nooning." So little time was wasted going back and forth to the camp, a hot lunch was brought out to the boys in the woods. Bricks were heated and lined wooden boxes in which the hot lunch was placed and carried out by sleigh.

Women generally were not allowed in camp unless they worked in the cook shack or were members of the cook's family. In this picture some townsfolk, or lumber baron Jonathan Boyce's family, may have arrived for a visit to the Houghton Lake camp.

A group of shanty-boys gathered for this photograph with their peaveys and cant hooks.

Oxen were generally used for skidding logs, while horses were used for heavy hauling. Occasionally when the camp ran short of meat, late in the winter, they butchered one of the oxen.

These men are skidding a fresh-cut log to a tote road or a nearby skidway where the logs will then be pulled by sled to the river banking grounds.

Often when the photographer would come into camp, the men would load a so-called "champion" load of logs and move them a short distance by horse-drawn sled. Almost every large camp claimed such a champion load. These sleds hauled the logs to the river or nearby narrow gauge railroad connections.

BOOMTOWN!

It is difficult to imagine the rapid growth that characterized Bay City and West Bay City in the halcyon years from 1868 to 1890. Decidedly a "boomtown," the combined populations grew from 4,000 in 1865 to 13,690 in 1874; 38,902 in 1884; and 40,820 by 1890! While statistics may create ambivalence, they do enable a picture of the town to emerge during this time of amazing growth. In 1884 a panoramic view of Bay City revealed 60 sawmills scattered along the river front. Drying stacks of pine boards piled high on each bank created a river canyon. Teepee burners belched smoke, and mounds of sawdust, bark, and cull lumber lined the river. The once clean river was brown and ugly, clogged with runoff, bark, splintered logs, and boards. Unpainted boardinghouses, saloons, and undulating docks and walkways could be seen jutting out between riverfront sawmills. Steamships and railroads ran everywhere. They carried boards, fish, and wood products southward; they brought immigrants northward. The quiet fishing villages, where the Trombleys once lived, had become industrial cities.

Of course, for many the boomtown era also brought with it unbounded confidence and prosperity. This was nowhere more apparent than in Bay City's exclusive residential districts. Nearly 80 percent of the city's resident lumber barons lived in a six-block area along Center Avenue. But behind these elegant homes were fine middle-class residences and many substantial working-class neighborhoods. Bay City's German and Polish immigrant laborers owned their own homes at rates that exceeded most other Michigan cities. Church spires rose almost as quickly as the trees fell, and peaceful, comfortable neighborhoods sprouted all over.

Workers and lumbermen prospered because of the sawmills, and much of that success came during the summer sawing months from May through October. The river system and the weight of the pine logs determined the seasonal pattern of the Great Lakes logging industry. The most costly task involved in logging was moving a 16- to 20-foot pine log from the interior to the sawmills. The easiest way to move a 300-pound log was to drag it out of the woods over hard-packed snow. Thus woods work was almost exclusively a winter-time operation. Snowfall was important not only to move the logs over iced tote roads, but enough run-off was needed in the spring to float logs down the rapidly-running rivers. As soon as the snow melted in the spring, logs that were stored on banking grounds or rollways, were tumbled into the rivers below. "River hogs" rode the logs downstream and kept the river free of jams and other obstructions. By late April the logs began to arrive at the rivertowns' sawmills.

Looking toward the Third Street Bridge about 1880. In the right hand corner is a white tent saloon owned by one of the Tierney brothers, and in the right center of photo two men sit in front of a passenger and freight boat dock where rates are posted.

View of Center Avenue looking east, c. 1880. This was probably taken from Saginaw Street; the First Baptist Church near the present day Masonic Temple, can be seen on the right. This is a good representation of Bay City in its lumber heyday.

The sawmills ran primarily during the summer months. In the peak years, as many as 10,000 men flooded Bay City from the logging camps to find work in the sawmills. These river mills were almost all constructed alike. The initial sawmills, built in the 1840s, were water-powered; but in 1845, the first steam-powered mill was built at the foot of Sixth Street. Steam sawmills were usually two-story buildings built close to the river. Steam power plants and heavy machinery to drive the saws were located on the first floor. Cutting was done on the second floor. Logs pulled up from river mill ponds were fed into circular saws or gang saws that ripped the logs into one inch-thick boards. Rough-sawn boards were edged and planed, then stacked on wharves along the river to dry and await shipment eastward. A "board foot"—12 x 12 inches and 1 inch thick—served as the standard of measurement.

The rapid growth and success of Bay City and West Bay City cannot be explained simply by location. "Necessity," it is said, "is the mother of invention;" and nowhere is this more evident than in the lumber-towns. The key reason for boomtown growth (and also the unanticipated rapid cutting of the forest interior) was the insatiable demand for lumber, which in turn was met with new inventions that sped up the entire process of turning trees into boards. Common predictions, from lumbermen and community boosters in the early 1870s, that there were enough trees to last several generations did not take into account the advent of faster saws and modern transportation.

In the space of one generation the sawmills moved from primitive sawing techniques, that often took a quarter of an hour to cut one board, to saws that were cutting three entire logs into boards in less than a minute. Before the Civil War the 19 or so

The mill pond in the foreground held a supply of logs to feed the saws usually located on the second floor of the sawmill. This photo is of McGraw's large sawmill in the South End.

Workers gather in front of a local mill with a giant circular saw blade. The saw blades were generally taken down and replaced with sharpened blades every three hours. The barrels on the roof hold water in case of fire or sparks from a nearby fire. The mill is the Hitchcock and Bialy sawmill at Cass on the Middle Grounds, 1882.

sawmills in Bay City ran the dangerous circular saw, the muley, and the sashsaw—an upright blade moving slowly within a frame. These were slow and wasteful—the kerf (or cut) was nearly one-quarter inch thick. The circular saw had a tendency to shatter and fire off chunks of metal at the operator. In the late 1860s an improved circular saw made of steel with curved sockets for the teeth, was much faster and safer. The gang saw, (built by Wickes Brothers in Saginaw and first used in Sage's mill) became the "monstrous giant of the mills." Twenty-four blades fastened in a frame enabled one log to be cut into several boards in one operation. Later the band saw was added which was faster and even less wasteful.

These new sawing techniques enabled sawmills in Bay City to grow to resemble industrial factories. Sage's, McGraw's, and other mills soon employed 300 or more workers each and turned out 40 million board feet of lumber a season. As the production of different grades of lumber became more sophisticated, subsidiary industries developed that took advantage of cheap and cull lumber to produce barrels, laths, woodenware, boxes, fence pickets and other items.

The other key development that accelerated growth and commercial-industrial prosperity was the modernization of transportation. Although plank roads continued to be built, lumbering relied foremost on waterborne transportation. Lumbermen frequently branched out into shipping and shipbuilding. They also slowly overcame their initial reluctance to build railroads, and by the peak years hundreds of miles of track radiated out of Bay City bringing in logs and shipping out finished lumber products.

"Big Wheels:" the first invention, in the 1870s, that sped up the work of getting the logs out of the woods. They provided for year 'round logging, were 12 to 14 feet in diameter, and often were put together by the camp blacksmith.

These men pose with one of the early steam locomotives used to haul logs from the interior to the banking grounds and sometimes, as probably represented here, directly to the sawmills. This was the second innovation, brought to Michigan in 1876, that accelerated the process of logging the interior.

Subsidiary Manufacturers

There were no booming grounds in Bay City. Most of the booming—separating the logs by log marks—was done in Saginaw. Henry Sage was an investor in the Au Gres Booming Company seen here in 1886. The men are holding pike poles.

Salt

The state bounty of 10 cents a bushel in 1859 prompted several speculators and lumbermen to investigate the process of producing salt from the vast supply of brine water located beneath the Saginaw Valley. Turning brine into salt merely required pumping and boiling away the brine water in large cast-iron kettles. As the water boiled away, salt crystallized along the edges where it would be scraped from each kettle, purified, and packed in wooden barrels. Sawdust, scrap lumber, and later steam and solar-heating methods were all used in Bay City to evaporate the brine.

Besides their attempt at Salzburg, Fraser, Fitzhugh, and Birney also sank a well along North Water Street. James McCormick and Judge Albert Miller sank salt wells in Portsmouth. There was plenty of brine and an abundance of cull lumber to boil away the brine. The cost of manufacturing salt in the valley was lower than in any other salt-producing area in the United States. Salt manufacturing soon became a profitable enterprise for lumbermen. Henry Sage estimated that his annual profits from salt production during the 1870s ranged from $25,000 to $30,000. Outside of lumbering, salt manufacturing employed more workers than any other operation in Bay City. In 1888 about one-quarter of all wage earners in the sawmills worked producing salt. There were 28 salt operations in Bay City in 1883, and it was estimated that "fully one half of the salt of the United States is made in the Saginaw Valley."

This success though did not come accidentally. Competition from New York manufacturers compelled lumbermen in Bay City and Saginaw to form the Saginaw and Bay City Salt Company. This cartel

Salt works in Bay City were the second largest employer behind the sawmills. In the 1870s the Saginaw Valley provided about one-half of the nation's salt.

handled 80 percent of the salt shipped from the valley and effectively controlled prices and regulated railroad shipping rates for salt. Renamed the Michigan Salt Association, it became a powerful, nationwide trust and set prices on everything from table salt to low-grade packing salt. It regulated costs by controlling all production and, when independents threatened prices, the association, as Sage wrote "would put the knife to the jugular and bleed all concerned til they were anxious for an arrangement." When the lumber industry declined in the 1890s, the cheap fuel supply was lost and salt operations closed down with the sawmills.

Above: This view of Bay City's northeast area, or "Dolsenville," along the river is marked by a series of brine wells seen projecting from various sawmills. Brine water was pumped from the wells and then boiled to leave the salt residue.

Below: Another method used to boil away the brine water was to use exhaust steam from the sawmill and carry it through pipes in pans of brine as seen here at the Bigelow-Cooper salt works, 1917.

Wood Products

A second spin-off industry from lumbering was the manufacturing of wood products. Early-on, cull lumber—boards rejected as poor quality—were left to be burned or cast into the river. By the 1870s, though, almost every sawmill began to manufacture useable products from scrap lumber. Laths for wall plaster, fence pickets, wooden boxes, and crates soon found ready markets. Later, hardwood was also used to make curtain rods, mop and broom handles, and kindling wood.

Several other wood-related products were also manufactured in Bay City. Planks and cedar and pine blocks were cut for paving streets and sidewalks. Roofing shingles of pine and cedar were also cut. The largest shingle mill in the valley—it produced nearly half of the county's shingles—was the J. R. Hall Mill in Essexville, along the river at the foot of Scheurmann Rd. While shingles could be cut in great quantities—6,000 per hour—by special, newly invented machines, the process was dangerous and a shingle maker could usually be readily identified by his missing fingers.

Bousfield Lumber mill. The Bousfield Company became the largest woodenware factory of its kind in the world in the 1880s. They made pails, tubs, churns, and all kinds of wooden shipping pails.

These are firemen and other workers at the Bois Mill in Essexville in 1895. The firemen tended the boilers that produced steam to power the mill equipment. Pictured here are Marsh Gulette, seated; Nicholas Neering, far right; and Tom Cole, second from right.

Wooden barrels made at a cooperage shop in Bay City. Most likely these were used locally for salt or fish packing. Shooks were unassembled barrels packaged and shipped from Bay City.

Woodenware works were also established early. These concerns produced washtubs, churns, pails, wooden bowls, and utensils. Bousfield and Company in Portsmouth, at the foot of 34th Street, became the largest such factory in the world in the 1880s.

Another rather unique concern in Bay City was the Northwestern Gas and Water Pipe Company located at the end of Madison Street on the present-day Chevrolet site. It manufactured hollowed wooden pipes and banded stave pipes for chemical and gas lines. Later called the Michigan Pipe Company, it remained in business until 1955.

As salt manufacturing and export fishing developed into major businesses in Bay City there was an accompanying demand for pine barrels to ship these products. Most of the sawmills that produced salt soon made their own pine barrels, but soon they expanded these operations into manufacturing ash, elm, and oak barrels for use in transporting fish, flour, nails, crackers, and liquids. The local barrel industry became so successful that by the 1880s "shooks"—unassembled barrels—were being shipped nationally. Barrel industry manufacturers spun-off to make wooden cisterns, water tanks, and wooden pipes.

Coopers gather for photo. Most sawmills that produced salt employed a number of men to manufacture barrels in the mill for salt packing.

Pitching with asphalt and sawdust wooden pipes at the Michigan Pipe Company located on the Powertrain property at the foot of Madison.

These men join two wooden, banded pipes. The Michigan Pipe Company continued in operation until 1955 and made pipe that lasted for many years.

Other wood-related industries in Bay City included sash and window-frame manufactures. This may be the Arnold and Catlin frame factory at Thomas and Linn streets.

SHIPBUILDING

Its location at the mouth of the Saginaw River, difficult overland transportation, and the industries of lumbering, logging, and fishing all made Bay City residents dependent on water transportation. It is not surprising, therefore, that there was a continuous demand for boats and ships of all kinds.

Initially small schooners, fishing boats, small sailing vessels, and canal boats were built of oak, pine and tamarack that was easily accessible. By the 1850s several larger steamboats were built along the Saginaw, but the industry actually began when Samuel J. Tripp opened a yard in Bay City (1856) and William Crosthwaite opened his shipyard and dry-dock in Banks around 1864. These firms and several other smaller operations built wooden tugs, yachts, and large sailing ships.

Captain James Davidson opened his shipyard at the corner of Fisher and Crump.

Schooner *Aberdeen* built at Davidson Shipyard, Bay City.

Frank W. Wheeler

Here a construction crew, sometimes of up to 500 men, shape a wooden hull in Frank W. Wheeler's dry-dock

In 1889 the Wheeler yard in West Bay City began making steel ships and—along with James Davidson, who opened his yard near the present-day Community Center in 1877—became one of the largest ship-builders on the entire Great Lakes. At one time Davidson's firm employed over 500 men and in 1889 Wheeler's work force numbered nearly 1,000. Both companies built some of the largest freighters to ply the Great Lakes.

These industries continued in operation until the early twentieth century. Labor unrest, poor management, and financial difficulties forced the Davidson shipyard to build little but scows after 1905 until it ceased building ships completely in 1915; the Wheeler yard, which had merged with the American Shipbuilding Company in Saginaw, continued as a supply and repair yard until 1908.

Above Left: Shipyard hands along North Water Street on the West Side.

Center Left: W. J. Ouellette's Boat Works, Bay City, built smaller Great Lakes' fishing and pleasure craft.

Above Right: James Davidson's new dry dock, November 1, 1900. Behind is the *Venezuela* and in dry dock the *Bermuda.*

Center Right: Ships built in Frank W. Wheeler's yard. *The Penobscot,* on the left and the *John Mitchell* in foreground.

Wrecks off Davidson yard. Older ships were burned and sunk at the Davidson yard rather than dismantled. There are six such ships visible at times of low water in the river.

River Commerce

It is difficult to overemphasize the vast amount of freight—lumber, salt, fish, and wood products—and passengers that shipped in and out of Bay City during the lumber era. By the 1880s the Saginaw Bay was easily the most active port on Lake Huron. Between 1879 and 1889 an average of 4000 vessels cleared port annually; during the peak six-month shipping season, 12 large ships went through Bay City daily.

Passenger transport records indicate that for $5 a person could depart the Saginaw River by one of four steamers leaving for Cleveland, Detroit and Toledo weekly. Regular lines served Tawas, Au Sable, Au Gres, and Port Austin; a boat left Bay City for Saginaw every two hours. The Boy Line's four ships made regular, inexpensive runs between Bay City and nearby towns. Later the *Metropolis, Arundell,* and the *Wellington R. Burt,* built with somewhat more comfortable accommodations, made frequent trips on

The *John Harrison,* a barge being pulled by tugboat, carries logs along the Saginaw River. This was one method of keeping Bay City's sawmills in operation by supplying logs from Canada.

Tug *Temple Emery* pulling the timber barge *Wahnipitae.* The *Wahnipitae* was wrecked in October, 1890, against the break-water in Cleveland.

The tugboat, *Howard,* owned by the Davidson Shipyards, is caught against the Third Street Bridge in 1914.

the river and excursions to points along Saginaw Bay.

Logging and lumbering also depended upon water transportation, and lumbermen financed the clearing of the Saginaw River to remove snags, obstructions and sand bars. The river was often deepened and wharves and docks constructed. As late as 1888, despite railroad construction, over three-quarters of all lumber, hardwoods, barrels, and woodenware products left the area by ship. Tugs, hauling schooners, freighters, pile-drivers, dredges, sailboats, steamboats, and passenger ships, plied the river. One of the most successful operators was Capt. Benjamin Boutell of Bay City, who worked the river for 39 years. His fleet of 21 tugs, several large transport ships and a work force of 500 men hauled timber and boards all over the Great Lakes. He often claimed that he owned "the largest and finest fleet of tugs in the world."

Named after Saginaw's wealthiest lumberman, the *Wellington R. Burt* was built in Carrollton in 1876. It was a sidewheel paddle steamer and took passengers between Bay City and Saginaw.

During the early years of shipping on the Great Lakes, the lighthouse at the mouth of the river was funded by subscription from shipowners. Julia Toby Brawn served as lighthouse keeper with her husband and then alone with the aid of a son from 1864 to 1890. She kept a vigil for years, refueling the lanterns and keeping the ever-present beacon operating for the sailors who depended on her for safety.

GREAT LAKES' FISHING CAPITAL

The Saginaw Bay has always been known for its commercial and sport fishing. Its warm, shallow waters and extensive wetlands made it a natural fish-spawning ground and seasonal migrations of sturgeon, herring, whitefish, and pickerel swarmed into the bay. James Fraser, the founder of Lower Saginaw, was one of the first settlers to encourage commercial fishing. In 1843 he opened a cooperage to make barrels to pack salted fish for export.

Any account of Saginaw Bay fishing begins with almost unbelievable statistics setting out the amount of fish caught "in the good old days." Indeed in 1850, "30 barrels of fish (sturgeon) were taken a day with spears;" in 1882, "60 tons of pickerel taken on April 7;" in 1937, "100 fishing boats in Bay City caught 2,795 tons of herring," and "the Saginaw Bay was once the fishing capital of inland America." Setting the numbers aside, one must imagine what the Banks area of the river looked like 100 years ago.

Fishing flourished in the spring and fall months. Every morning, shortly after dawn, hundreds of men set out in small wooden boats to harvest their catches. In the early years, seine nets were popular. These were essentially net fences strung out for hundreds of feet and held up by stakes driven into the bay bottom. Pound nets, used until the 1920s, consisted of a large pot or holding area that fish were led into by two long net-like leads. They were strung out like seines. These were replaced in some cases by trap nets in the 1920s. In the summer months, Banks' river edge would be lined with nets that had been pulled ashore. Men, not working in sawmills, would hose their nets down, dry them, and treat them with a tar preservative. Nets were mended and then stored in sheds

W. P. Sharp was a pioneer commercial fisherman in Essexville in the late nineteenth century.

W. P. Sharp's promotional card.

until the fall season began. In November, during the stormiest month of the year, crews would pull the stakes and once-again haul in the nets. Hired fishermen earned about $1 a day in peak seasons.

In the early years fish were salted and packed in pine barrels to be carried by ship to Great Lakes markets. In 1864, Harvey Williams began packing fresh fish in ice cut from the bay. Fish were stored in "freezers," usually at the mouth of the river. When the railroads arrived the exports of fresh fish rapidly increased. Along the wharves in Banks, rails and roads ran parallel to the river and in the early afternoon buyers eagerly awaited the day's catch. Tons of fish were bid upon, bought, quickly packed in barrels, and transferred by wagon or truck to nearby railroad yards. No packed fish were allowed to stay in Bay City overnight.

The number of fish in the bay began to decline in the 1930s, and commercial fishing all but disappeared by the late 1950s. Most fishermen attribute the destruction of the Saginaw Bay fishery to a number of things, overfishing not being one of these factors. "If overfishing was the reason," one fisherman said recently, "then now, with curtailment of the fisheries, the fish would be so thick that you could walk across the bay." Ecological changes brought on by heavy pollution during the war years destroyed the fish-spawning grounds. There were no controls over what companies could dump into the rivers. The sea lamprey dealt the final blow to lake trout, herring, and other fish. Lastly over-enrichment of the bay by phosphate detergents, fertilizers, insecticides, and herbicides all contributed to ruined spawn beds. Although today sport fishing has been revived on the bay, commercial fishing, a way of life for generations of fishermen, has been lost forever.

Unloading fish at the mouth of the Saginaw River in Bay City.

Tending fishing nets in 1930 in Essexville. The nets were repaired usually in the summer months for the fall season.

Commercial fishing activity at the mouth of the Saginaw river.

Railroads Came Slowly to the Bay Cities

For almost 30 years after Lower Saginaw was laid out as a paper village, townspeople had to depend on water routes for most transportation needs. The state of Michigan never enthusiastically supported internal railroad construction after losing money in early state-sponsored ventures in 1850. Private and local capital was necessary to carry on railroad building. People with money, especially the lumbermen in Bay City, were slow in promoting railroads. Logging was largely dependent on water related transportation and lumbermen had invested heavily in ships, barges, and schooners. They were reluctant to have local investors finance competition. Likewise, steam engines threw off sparks that caused prairie and forest fires that often burnt valuable timber lands.

Bay City businessmen and some lumbermen began to agitate for a railroad after East Saginaw completed a railroad connection to Flint in 1862. These efforts were tempered by those in town who stated that it was virtually impossible to build a roadbed through the swamps between Bay City and East Saginaw. After three years of planning and internal opposition, the editor of the *Bay City Journal* expressed his frustration with the lack of progress:

> Do the people of this city think that business prospects of a road to this point are sufficient to induce some company to build it without any effort being made here? If so, we shall continue to travel through mud and mire to reach the outer world. Call a meeting to stir up people, something, anything, everything, rather than sit down in the mud as we have been doing for years past.

The county board of supervisors soon appropriated $75,000 to aid the privately financed East Saginaw and Bay City Railroad Company. In early 1866 the board expressed its dissatisfaction to railroad president James Birney, Jr. that little was being done and threatened to withdraw its appropriation unless the line was graded by the end of the year. Apparently that threat had an effect, for in January, 1866, Birney advertised for railroad ties and hired A. S. Munger to supervise construction. The railroad bed was built on dredgings from a canal dug through the swamps and completed to East Saginaw in November 1867. At a celebratory inauguration ban-

The crew of the Michigan Central's Engine 113 in Bay City. The first locomotives were woodburners with huge smokestacks and shields over the stacks to cut the spread of sparks.

Michigan Central Railroad: Snowplow Engine and crew in northern Michigan.

quet, Munger was given a $350 gold watch in appreciation of his work. The 12-mile spur was financed completely by private contributions and Bay County.

Movement in Bay City prompted Wenona to develop, as the *Journal* reported, a case of "railroad on the brain." Henry Sage, his partner John McGraw, and Salzburg investor Daniel Fitzhugh contracted with the Jackson, Lansing and Saginaw Railroad at Saginaw City to build an extension along the west side of the river to Wenona. The lumbermen agreed to build the line in exchange for $80,000 in railroad stock. More support came from a village bond to finance railroad improvements in Wenona. Sage pressured the board of supervisors to construct new slips and public docks along the river as an integral part of the railroad network. Without great expense to himself, Sage managed to get the railroad built to his company town. The line was completed in January, 1868, and gave Wenona connections to Saginaw City, Owosso, Lansing, and Chicago. Sage also saw the importance of West Side connections north and west and hinted that he would help finance future extensions. These lines into the interior, where Sage owned valuable pinelands, would boost property values and stimulate trade for his company stores in Wenona.

By the 1880s West Bay City and Bay City had important railroad connections running along Lake Huron northward and westward to Midland. In 1873 the Michigan Central—which had taken over the Jackson, Lansing and Saginaw line—built a bridge across the river and made connections to Detroit via Vassar. In 1876, the Michigan Central had extended this line north to Mackinac City; and in 1888 completed a spur line to Midland from West Bay City.

Railroad travel was far less comfortable in the late nineteenth century than it is in romanticized memories. Travel was slow—about 25 to 35 miles an hour—over uneven, undulating roadbeds in uncomfortable coaches. A three hour trip to Detroit in 1900 on a Pere Marquette day coach is described by one traveler as "dirty, sooty, and crowded with tired mothers, fretty children, and lunch boxes." The fare to Detroit was listed at $2.18; but if you could afford a parlor car, the ride was more enjoyable in wide, plush seats, porter service and time to enjoy the "fields, farmhouses, and the tiny villages along the way."

Officials of the railroad, crew and passengers disembark from railroad car in Bay City.

New York Central's (Michigan Central) Inspection Locomotive "Cleveland" at Bay City.

Steam Locomotive Engine 3 of the Detroit Bay City and Western Railroad, engineer and fireman.

CHAPTER 4: LUMBERTOWN LIFE

The Aldelphi Theater
Men congregate here in an atmosphere thick with tobacco smoke to guzzle beer and whiskey, listen to vile jokes, and to watch brazen women as they leer and smirk and kick up their heels in the can-can. In the wine room, for admission to which 50 cents extra is charged, the girls mingle freely with the men, who go there to see them and drink.
                                  Bay City Observer, April 5, 1877

It was from these small, out-of-the-way railway stations in the interior that shanty boys purchased the infamous "ticket to hell," to return to the lumbertowns for the spring bender and summer sawmill work. Note the sign: "Danger! Look out for mail pouches thrown from train at this point."

This is looking down Bay City's Water Street, c. 1888, toward what was often called "hell's half-mile." At Third Street and Water were the Catacombs, a collection of saloons and brothels that the shanty boys came to each spring.

LUMBERTOWN ENTERPRISE

The "ticket to hell" is what the shanty boys called it, and it was often a ticket to Bay City. When the northern logging camps closed down in the spring, the hands were paid off. They wandered out of the woods, purchased a train ticket at a small, byway rail station and set out for one of the booming lumbertowns. Though there were exceptions, tradition testified that almost every shanty boy's stake was spent in a week of drinking, carousing, and revelry. When his money was nearly gone, he headed home to the farm or hooked up with a local sawmill for summer employment.

Though Bay City's newspapers and church people periodically condemned this "yearly torrent of wickedness," they did little to stop it. In reality, the presence of the raucous shanty boys was good for many businesses. Thousands of dollars were to be made off the "foolish and innately thriftless shanty boy." To take advantage of this annual windfall, additional businesses sprouted. The saloon was the most obvious enterprise that catered to the visiting lumberjack, but there were many other less conspicuous dance halls, gambling dens, resorts, and brothels. There were also less vile businesses. Restaurants, jewelry stores, clothing stores, boardinghouses, and hotels all served these transient workers. Entrepreneurs devised more than one way to tap the shanty boy and mill worker of his hard-earned wages.

As enterprising Bay City grew larger, additional people were attracted to the boomtown. Not only did lumberjacks often find permanent work and homes in town, but a sizeable middle class developed because of lumbertown support services. Although most of these city dwellers invested their savings in homes, businesses or industries, many citizens were also willing to subscribe time and money to improve municipal services. Fire protection, law enforcement, medical care, and good government are examples of the most pressing needs, but others, like churches, schools and libraries were also necessary to bring stability and civilization to this raucous frontier and industrial boomtown.

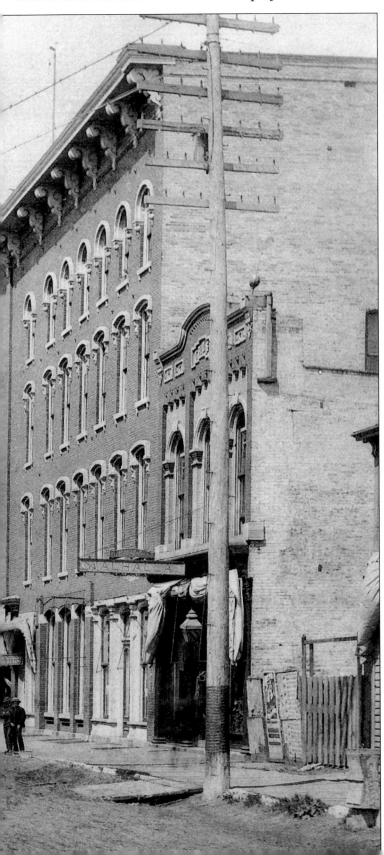

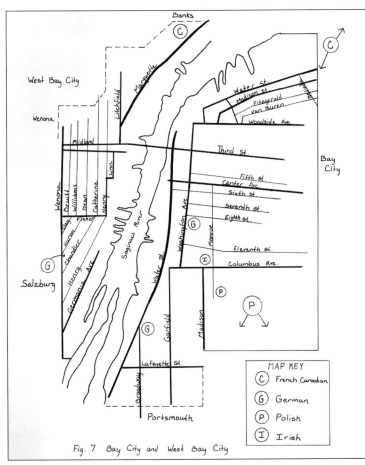

Map of Bay City and West Bay City depicting the towns and areas of settlement by various immigrant groups, 1890.

Town Growth and Settlement Patterns

Once commerce and industry were established, Bay City and West Bay City began to grow, and the permanent physical shape of the town was determined. Bay City, as it grew, was engaged in competition for settlers not only with her cross-river rival but also with her downriver neighbor. After Bay City changed its name from Lower Saginaw in 1857, efforts were made to incorporate the village of Portsmouth into Bay City in 1859. Water Street was connected with its counterpart in Portsmouth and streets were planned to integrate the two communities. However, when Bay City was chartered as a city in 1865, Portsmouth was not included. It was united with Bay City in 1873. In the meantime Bay City continued to expand its grid-street pattern eastward at right angles from the river in contrast to Portsmouth, which followed a traditional north-south grid arrangement. Between these two settlements a conflicting street layout developed and the area was settled haphazardly.

Across the river, Wenona grew steadily after incorporating as a village in 1867. Sage's company town expanded by integrating plats of various speculators who built residential subdivisions adjacent to the company's original 116 acres. From 1871 to 1875, especially after Bay City annexed Portsmouth in 1873, efforts were made to convince Banks, Wenona, and Salzburg to join Bay City. Sage and residents on the West Side resisted, however, fearing higher taxes because of the need for inevitable West Side improvements. In 1877 the state legislature approved a plan to consolidate the three West Side towns into West Bay City. Though a rivalry emerged, West Bay City remained a smaller, less developed settlement, never competing vigorously with its larger, cross-river neighbor.

The most obvious change associated with the phenomenal growth of Bay City was the altered physical appearance of the town brought on by industrialization. The spatial structure of the town, which now came to look more like a modern industrial city, influenced people's perception of the community. As in the present, when we debate the character of Bay City's waterfront, physical appearance often defines the image, lifestyle, and the extent to which citizens involve themselves in townlife.

Despite the efforts of town boosters to paint an attractive town landscape, and drawings depicting idyllic bird's-eye views of a thriving industrial and

View of Saginaw River in Bay City from atop Michigan Pipe Works. Logs in the foreground are in a millpond waiting cutting. The lumber industry contributed to considerable river pollution as is evident in this photo.

Bay City from the West Side. This photo was taken at the end of the lumber era. Abandoned docks and cull lumber mark the riverfront. Little attention was paid to river beautification after lumbering, although some attempts were made to improve the town's downtown and its neighborhoods.

commercial center, Bay City was not necessarily a universally attractive settlement. From the waterfront, a newcomer could look over an industrial area of sawmills, shingle mills, shipyards, breweries, tanneries and fish factories. The river had long lost its clarity. Log rafts, bark, and brine run-off polluted the waterway and ran out into the bay. The sounds of whirling saws and the odor of burning wood confronted the senses often day and night.

Bay City's physical layout came to resemble a larger, distinctively urban landscape. Because lumbering was entirely dependent on water transportation, sawmills and woodworking industries were located along the river. Though a few non-related industries were located away from the Saginaw River—clothing, cigar manufacturers and breweries—almost all subsidiary industries were crowded within a few blocks of the water. These factories early-on destroyed the river banks—the one outstanding natural geographic attraction Bay City possessed.

Stores, saloons, and restaurants were the main types of establishments in the commercial districts. The commercial center in Bay City extended along Water, Saginaw, and Washington streets between Third Street to the north and Sixth Street to the south. Many of the general merchants, clothiers, jewelers, and dry goods stores were along Washington and Center. City offices were in the downtown commercial blocks as were several hotels. Because the river formed a bend around downtown Bay City, the commercial center was hemmed in on two sides by sawmills, fisheries, and woodworking industries. At the Portsmouth settlement, a few commercial establishments were located along Water Street. In West Bay City, a small business section built up along Midland and Linn streets. Sage sold lots in his original plat and financed several entrepreneurs in building commercial blocks. Choice locations along Midland Street sold for more than $1,000 by the late 1870s.

Characteristic of many nineteenth-century cities, areas of vice—saloons, dance halls, and brothels—were permitted in the downtown. Bay City's "Catacombs" developed such a reputation for prostitution, murder, and robbery that even today it is difficult to separate fact from fiction. In the early 1880s there were 26 hotels, 30 saloons, and 2 liquor stores located in a four block area along Water and Third streets. The name "Catacombs" was derived from the underground basements and passageways beneath the sidewalks that connected various saloons and resorts. During the spring townspeople seldom ventured into the Catacombs; certainly "proper" women

Washington and Center avenues looking south, c. 1886. The site of the Westover Opera House is at bottom right and the Phoenix Building is under construction.

Shearer Block, c.1888. The Jarmin & Vail store was on the northwest corner of Center and Adams.

These photos represent images of Bay City during its heyday. After 1890, the population fell and businesses frequently moved in and out of downtown locations.

remained well outside its boundaries. Yet, because it was actually a mixture of hotels, boardinghouses, restaurants, and barbershops—as well as saloons and brothels—it would be a mistake to conceptualize the Catacombs as an isolated and rigid area of vice. During the rest of the year a relative calm prevailed in the area.

Also, by the early 1880s patterns of residential segregation had developed in Bay City. Outside of saloons and resorts, the most prominent feature that a visitor would notice were the mansions built by resident lumbermen and wealthy manufacturers. As in most nineteenth-century industrial cities, families of greater means lived near the center of town. Center Avenue remains to this day a promenade characterized by elegant residences. Directly behind the mansions, merchants and professionals built their homes. Fifth and Sixth streets, which ran on each side of Center Avenue, contained many large if somewhat less ostentatious homes. Next, as one moved away from Center Avenue, were the homes of skilled workers and small businessmen.

Working-class residential areas were located along the river and beyond these Center Avenue residences.

The A. Neering Hardware Store was an example of the neighborhood businesses scattered throughout Bay City. Neering's was located on Woodside in Essexville.

Interior of a Bay City women's clothing store. The lumberjacks often patronized these stores after the winter cutting season and purchased items of clothing as gifts for wives and girl friends. Bay City had several millinery manufacturing businesses that also made clothes for men and women.

Meeker and Adams Grocery Store was located downtown on North Water and supplied various food items and supplies to shanty boys and camp bosses. Meeker and Adams was established in 1871.

William Galarno's General store was located on Belinda and Woodside streets. Mr. Galarno is standing in the doorway of the store. He began the business in 1874 and was a popular politician and merchant in the "Frenchtown" area.

The influx of immigrant workers in the 1870s created concentrated immigrant populations as most newcomers sought low-cost housing close to their place of employment. Sawmills often hired hands who lived nearby, thereby encouraging the growth of residential ethnic enclaves. Few lumbertowns had ethnic residential boundaries as well defined as Bay City's.

The original French populations continued to live near the mouth of the river and fish, or work in the nearby Dolsen, Chapin and Company sawmill. German workers concentrated along Eighth Street in Bay City and in Salzburg on the West Side. Five sawmills in Salzburg were run by and employed German millhands. In the early 1870s Polish settlers arrived in Bay City and settled in the extreme south end (Portsmouth); many were hired at John McGraw's sawmill along Water Street. Irish laborers, although not as large in number as the above groups, began to settle along Columbus, and a small Swedish settlement originated on the West Side between Salzburg and Wenona. Precise geographical boundaries, churches, schools, and nearby employment reinforced ethnic residential segregation in Bay City well beyond the lumber era.

Madison Park: Note the wooden sidewalks. This was one of the original parks laid out in Lower Saginaw by Fraser and James Birney in 1843 and became part of the German settlement on the east side.

Jackson Street looking north from 9th. Birney Park would be to left of photographer. This is an excellent picture of homes businessmen and professionals lived in off Center Avenue, a short walk from downtown.

A panoramic view of Center Avenue looking west, toward town, from Lincoln Street, 1888. Large homes with spacious yards and trees made Center Avenue the most prestigious address in town.

LUMBERTOWN SALOONS

Every spring, as soon as a trainload of shanty boys arrived at the station, "runners," hired by individual saloons, met each man and offered wooden nickels or other incentives to entice the woodsman to one particular saloon. There were plenty to choose from. In 1880 when Bay City had nearly 27,000 residents, 162 saloons opened day and night in the city and another 26 operated on the West Side. The Bay City taverns that the men trekked to ranged in respectability from dark and dank grog shops to more inviting places where a free lunch might be set out. There were also neighborhood saloons where family men gathered every evening and some elegant, carefully decorated parlors that served businessmen.

While the saloons in the Catacombs were disreputable places and often catered to prostitutes and gamblers, a good many of the saloons in Bay City grew out of the need for fellowship and a home-away-from-home. A clear glass of beer, for one, was often better after a hard day's work than polluted city water—where a fish might drop from the faucet—or a drink from a contaminated backyard well. The neighborhood saloon in Bay City provided immigrant male workers a place to enjoy fellowship, grab a free sandwich, play a game of cards, read a foreign-language newspaper, or learn about seasonal job offerings. Saloonkeepers often cashed workers' checks or lent them small sums of money when they were short. Taverns became meeting places for politicians, ethnic clubs, and trade unions. French fishermen, German and Polish millhands, railroad workers, and ship builders all had their favorite hangouts in Bay City. In short the nineteenth century, working-class saloon often provided a male retreat from the cares of daily life.

These men pose in front of the Lion Saloon. Most neighborhood drinking places were plain, simple buildings that frequently changed ownership. Bay City had 162 such places in 1880.

The Two Johns Saloon was a somewhat better drinking place and survived into the 1890s. Saloonkeepers were often well-known to their clients and served as bankers and money lenders to sawmill workers who needed cash toward the end of the month.

Advertisement for the New European Hotel at Third and Water streets. This building is present-day St. Laurent's Nut House and, because of its location, was one of the most popular workingman's hotels in town. The original notorious brothel here was gutted by fire and then converted to the "New European."

Interior of the New European Hotel. The hotel was in the heart of the Catacombs area, but in the post-lumber era acquired a somewhat better reputation as seen by its clientele in this photo. Note the blurred dog moving across the right foreground. Taken in June, 1909.

Resorts, Dance Halls, and Variety Theaters

Resorts, dance halls, and variety theaters were all essentially facades for places of prostitution. Prostitution was also closely associated with the saloon business. It should be remembered that prostitution may be immoral, but in the nineteenth-century it was not illegal. While the hundreds of women engaged in the trade usually worked from one of the scores of saloons along Third and Water streets, dance halls, variety theaters, and some restaurants also provided female companionship. The third floor of the building that today houses St. Laurent Bros.' peanut house at Third and Water served as an emporium and theater. Admission to the third floor theater was $5, more costly than the common dives along Water Street, but "where the plays presented were suited to the most vilest and depraved taste."

Saloonkeepers, businessmen and law enforcement officers did little to regulate prostitution because it was good for business. Shanty boys came into town with a winter's wage of between $150 and $200, and most residents saw prostitution as a small impropriety as long as it brought in its associated revenue. During the peak crime months of 1884—May and June according to Bay City police arrest records—there were probably as many as 300 "pretty waiter girls" engaged in prostitution. In time there were more permanent, or luxurious houses, discreetly located south along Water Street and in older homes throughout the city. "Ma Smith" ran a home of 12 to 20 girls on Water Street, and even the town marshal in 1875, D. H. McCraney, owned a brothel where he reputedly spent most of his time. Polly Dickson was a popular "dancer" in the Catacombs; Maggie Shay, Kissing Jennie, and Morphine Lou were other well-known prostitutes who frequented the Do-Drop-Inn or the Idaho Saloon on Water Street. The latter girl's name was reflective of the availability of legal drugs, purchased from apothecary shops, that often "hooked" young women into prostitution.

Gus Jaeger's Saloon was located at 606 N. Water, and was part of the two dozen or so establishments that were within "Hell's Half Mile."

This is an interior view of an unidentified Bay City saloon. The bar and the mirror were the most expensive decorations. Taxes on saloons in Bay City ranged from $25 to $100 each in various years, but usually paid for most of Bay City's public services.

This young boy, who probably tagged along with his father, indicates that neighborhood saloons were often homes-away-from-home for workers and provided fellowship as well as a drink.

This is a rare picture of prostitutes who worked in Bay City and then moved north to Meredith to work for Julia Putnam. Prostitution was legal in Michigan until World War I.

Hotels and Boardinghouses

Hotels predated saloons in Bay City. The seasonal influx of traders, trappers, fishermen, and shanty boys prompted the construction of the Globe Hotel in Lower Saginaw in 1837; this was soon followed by the Center House in Portsmouth. Hotels that served the well-to-do customer were built even during the early days of the lumber boom and reached their peak with the construction of the Fraser House in 1865 on the site of Delta College's planetarium. The Fraser was gutted by fire in 1906, but was quickly replaced by the luxurious Wenonah Hotel in 1908. In 1977 the Wenonah also burned in a tragic conflagration that took nine lives.

Because of large transient populations engaged in the occupations of lumbering, fishing, and shipbuilding, hotels were built in Bay City in greater numbers than residents would normally need. In 1887 the *Bay City Tribune* noted that in both cities there were 81 hotels with accommodations for 6,000 people. Establishments in Bay City catered to people of all tastes. The Wolverton House at Third and Water at one time a fine hotel, eventually became associated with the Catacombs' illicit activities. The Forest City House, Saginaw and Sixth, became known as the "German hotel;" the Portland House at Washington and First, was the stagecoach's stopover accommodation; and the Republic Hotel was famous as the winter home of Great Lakes sea captains and a gathering place for politicians.

There were plenty of cheap hotels that were often worse than milltown boardinghouses and offered little more than a shared room and a straw-filled mattress. Company and privately owned boardinghouses supplemented the hotels and supplied shelter to single male workers as well as single women. There were eight boardinghouses for women along Water Street and ten more on Woodside between Adams and Jefferson streets. Most of these residents were "pretty waiter girls" who worked the saloons along Water Street.

Near the sawmills, common two- or three-story "railroad" boardinghouses, 30 x 80 feet, were quickly constructed. It usually cost $5 or $6 per week for room and board. Perhaps the most notorious tenement blockhouse was Henry Sage's, "the Barracks" in Wenona. This den of "rats, mice, cockroaches, bedbugs, and lice," invited social ostracism for any family living there. The building was destroyed by an arsonist in 1875. After the lumber business declined and later railroad traffic disappeared, most of the downtown hotels closed.

The Portland House Hotel served as Bay City's stop for the stagecoach that ran between the city and Midland. It was located on the northeast corner of Washington and First streets, and rooms rented for $1 to $1.25 per night. This is an interesting photo considering the number of people gathered here and that they are a better dressed clientele, c. 1880-85.

The Franklin House Hotel was located on the northeast corner of Sixth and Water streets.

This is the Maple Grove Hotel on Center and Park streets. It burned in 1899. Fred Metzger, and Carrie, Rose, and Martha Metzger are pictured along the wooden access road.

The Astor House Hotel was considered the "principal hotel" on the city's South End at Harrison and Cass near the river. This is an 1887 photo; the hotel opened in 1873.

The Republic Hotel was not torn down until the late 1960s. It served, at Fourth and Saginaw, as the winter home for Great Lakes captains and later was the gathering place for city politicians. The Republic's bar won a gold medal for its beauty at the Chicago exposition in 1893, then was relocated here later that year.

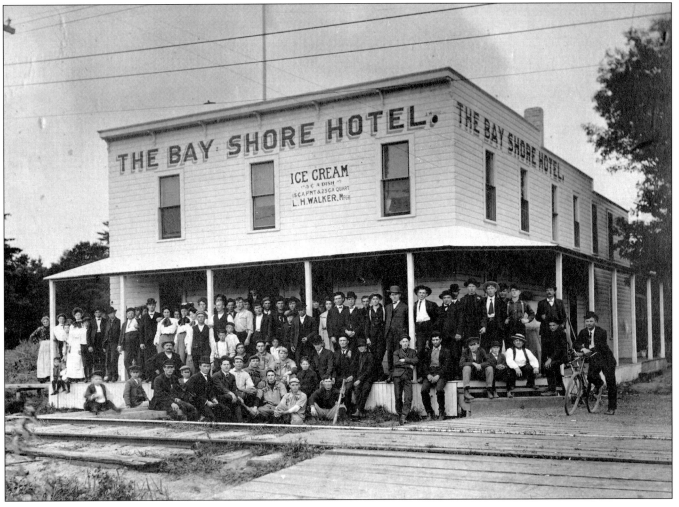

The Bay Shore Hotel at 56 State Park drive, was a popular stopping off spot for excursionists to the bay's beaches. The Kolb Bros. Baseball team is part of the group in front.

The Lefevre Hotel, torn down in 1979, was located at First and Jackson. It was across the street from the old Michigan Central Depot and was a popular place for workers and passengers on the line. A good number of railroad men also stayed at the Lefevre.

The New Clifton was a popular West Bay City hotel at 819 E. Midland Street. Note the men and women in the windows getting into the photograph.

Smith's European Hotel and Restaurant was more typical of the small establishments that catered to transient workers and single men and women. It was at Third and Washington streets just beyond the "Catacombs."

Interior of the Wenonah Hotel. When it was opened in 1908, the Wenonah was described "as palatial in all appointments." It was built as a replacement for the Fraser House which burned on Christmas Eve, 1906, and was located on the present site of the Delta College Planetarium.

A mosaic bust of Princess Wenonah was set in the lobby floor of the new Wenonah. When the Wenonah burned in 1977, the mosaic ended up in a rural farm field after demolition. It was later rescued and placed in the remodeled City Hall.

The grand Wenonah Hotel in its prime around 1924. The Bay City Grocers and Butchers annual meeting was being held here, and during these years customers were often turned away because of the hotel's popularity. A year later, 1925, a three-story addition increased accommodations to 244 rooms.

HOW VIOLENT WAS BAY CITY IN THE LUMBER ERA?

Although frequently ignored by historians and in popular literature as part of the Wild West, the lumbertowns—and Bay City especially—can be said to have been as wicked as their cowtown counterparts. Even local accounts that often appear to exaggerate Bay City's notorious past, are probably not out of line in light of recent research. Like the cowtowns that flourished in the same decades (1868-1888), the lumbertowns do indeed deserve their unsavory reputations.

Bay County Jail. While it looks rather tranquil from the outside, the jail, built in the late 1860s, stood for 70 years. It housed horse and cattle thieves, drunks, prostitutes, arsonists, murderers, and gamblers from the lumber era and bootleggers from the 1920s. The old building became a dangerous and forbidding firetrap and was replaced around 1937, after several escape attempts.

Bay City especially stood out for its tolerance of and association with vice and violence. The Catacombs attracted special attention and was written up in a contemporary *Police Gazette* exposé. The town marshal owned a house of prostitution. And because it was often the first railroad stop for woodsmen returning from the north every spring, Bay City attracted more than its share of thirsty and anxious shanty boys. Out-of-town newspapers frequently enhanced this reputation by referring in print to Bay City as "Tramp Heaven" or "Bum City."

One form of violence that separated Bay City from its western counterparts was "brawling." "Free fights" were common among 20 or 30 jacks, and these "friendly" battles often ended in injury and death. Irish shanty boys were known to move upon the Forest City Hotel and demand a go-'round with its German jacks. Records of the Bay City police in the 1880s were enscribed with scores of "assault and battery" charges every Sunday and Monday. Evidently, weekends were made for fighting in Bay City.

Prostitution in Bay City flourished in numbers well beyond the small red-light districts that were permitted in towns like Abilene or Dodge City, Kansas. One-quarter of lumbertown homicides were generally associated with prostitution in one way or another.

People were killed in Bay City during the lumber heyday, but not as often as they were out West. In the 20-year lumber era, 24 known homicides occurred in Bay County. This would be a rate comparable to modern-day killings. Few of these deaths, in fact, actually involved lumberjacks. Private confrontations, robbery, poisoning, infanticide, patricide, jealousy and many other unknown causes contributed to these murders. There were also a number of unclaimed "floaters," or bodies found along the river banks, that would inflate these statistics.

Few of the perpetrators were sent to prison. Fifty-six percent of those individuals involved in a killing were never punished. Tolerance, corrupt police forces, and economics all contributed to a fairly permissive attitude. After all, shanty boys—with their seasonal stake—did not come to towns where the authorities were too rough on them. In general considering prostitution, fighting, and rowdyism, Bay City fit well into the frontier tradition of violence.

"A DEAD YEAR"
[HEADLINE, *BAY CITY TRIBUNE*, JANUARY 1, 1884]

— 1 unknown floater found in river, May 27, 1883
— 1 suicide, July 12, 1883
— 1 body found floating in river, July 12, 1883
— 2 bodies found floating in river, July 15, 1883
— 1 unknown body in river, July 27, 1883
— 1 unknown floater, September 2, 1883
— 1 accidental shooting, September 21, 1883
— 1 suicide, crazy man leaped from hospital window, November 24, 1883
— 1 man kills another with club, December 21, 1883

Research of the newspapers for the year 1883—the height of the lumber era—revealed the above causes of deaths in Bay City.

LAW ENFORCEMENT IN THE LUMBER TOWNS

In the frontier era, Bay City's law enforcement was sporadic, uneven, and often enforced by volunteers on vigilance committees. The shanty boys, sailors, and traders, and sometimes Indians, who descended upon the town, eventually created a need for more consistent law enforcement. Bay County first elected a sheriff in 1857, and a village marshal was appointed in 1859. In 1873 Bay City's police force numbered 14 men.

The village of Bay City enacted early ordinances against "gaming and other lewd curiosities," but the formation of a vigilante group in Portsmouth in 1865 indicated the need for citizen participation to quell violence associated with the arrival of the shanty boys that spring.

Most of Bay City's budget went to pay fire wardens and to purchase fire-fighting equipment. Since less than 10 percent of the town's expenditures went to police work, little could be expected of the city force. In 1880 Bay City had one officer per 2,222 inhabitants. Low pay and physical and political harassment deterred most solid citizens from becoming police officers. Most policemen were hired based on size and their ability to quell bar fights among lumberjacks. In the winter months officers were often laid off.

In 1881, after Marshal McCraney was accused of blackmail, drunkenness and running a brothel, and nine policemen were discharged for various crimes, a revised city charter established a metropolitan system of police organization in Bay City. An independent Board of Police Commissioners was appointed to manage the new department. Since 1881 the professionalization of the department brought better pay, organization, and a higher caliber of policemen. After the two cities were consolidated in 1905, the advent of the automobile, and the decline of lumbering changed the nature of law enforcement as traffic control and parking regulation became added responsibilities.

Bay City policemen gather in front of old City Hall on Saginaw Street near Fifth, c. 1888. Despite its apparent size in this photo, keep in mind that the city's population was almost as large as today's. The police force was often undermanned in the lumber era.

Bay City police pose "formally" in front of the newly completed City Hall, c. 1900. The department professionalized in the 1880s and began wearing uniforms and receiving better pay.

After the turn of the century, the police department gradually became more involved in traffic and parking control in Bay City. This is a 1945 photograph of the city's traffic patrol and police cars.

Taken in the mid 1880s, this photo depicts the department shortly after reorganization. The professionalization of police was taking place in all major cities in the decade and generally consisted of the appointment of a non-political Board of Commissioners, uniforms for police, and some training.

Fire Department

When Bay City and West Bay City developed into important lumber centers, sawmills and drying stacks of wood located along the waterfronts were under constant threat of fire. Moreover, pine boards were widely used in construction of newer homes and businesses. A small fire could quickly ignite whole sections of the town; both cities had their share of spectacular blazes. The first formal fire-fighting company was formed in 1859.

In most communities it required one or two large fires before authorities took action to build up their fire departments. Bay City was no exception. Major conflagrations in 1863 and 1865 compelled the community to appoint H. M. Bradley, a sawmill owner, as the first fire chief and purchase a steam-powered fire engine. By 1868 there were three fire stations: the Neptune downtown, the Red Rover in the north end of town, and the Protective Association No. 2 at Tenth and Water streets. West Bay City was protected by the Active Company No. 5. By 1910, after the cities consolidated, there were ten stations.

Most early companies were volunteer fire brigades that paid the firemen between $25 and $35 a year. Some were manned full time, and, in addition to the low wages, firemen received free

Captain George Wauless, of the First Ward, Company No. 2, posing for a formal studio portrait. Because of the need to protect the sawmills, Bay City spent a good deal of money on and developed a strong sense of pride in their fire department. Considerably more money was expended on fire protection than law enforcement.

room and board. In time fire wardens were hired to keep watch and, by the mid 1870s, crews were kept full-time in every firehouse. Each company had several teams of horses, often kept in harness, and took pride in their teams' speed. However, there was always a problem with manpower, and at times when the horses were unhitched or hitched to another wagon there was no one around to harness the steam pumper.

Between 1911 and 1923 horse-drawn pumpers and wagons were replaced by fire trucks. The force grew to 125 fire fighters in 1968 and eight fire stations. By late twentieth century there were 58 men working four stations—two on each side of the river.

Bay City's hose wagon, Company No. 1 on left, and Company No. 2 on the right. About 90 percent of the tax monies collected from saloon fees went to purchase new equipment for the fire companies. Here the firemen display a hose wagon, c. 1880s.

"Active" Fire Company on Morton Street on the southwest side near the old Wolverine Bean site. Fire companies acquired descriptive names as well as numbers to tell them apart. Bay City had the "Red Rover," "Protective," and the "Neptune' companies.

First Ward, Company No. 2, hose wagon decorated for parade. Standing in front, with silver trumpet, is Captain George Wauless.

Edward J. Cook, last fire chief of West Bay City, before city consolidation of the fire departments in 1907.

Chief E. J. Cook seated on Fire Chief's carriage used to speed to fires. Cook retired in 1911 after injuries suffered in the Watson Block fire a year earlier.

Fire Station No. 6 was located on the southeast corner of 7th and Johnson streets, c. 1905. The tower had an alarm bell that alerted the firemen and told them the general location of the fire. One long-time resident remembers; "The horse-drawn fire engines from station No. 6 used to race up and down McKinley night and day."

This is the Banks area firehouse. The men took pride in their horse teams and had them well trained. The horses and wagons were often included in early photos.

A new fire truck at Company No. 1 headquarters. The first fire trucks were purchased in 1911 and all the horse-drawn wagons were replaced by 1923. Note the tire chains on both vehicles. Fire trucks also permitted the consolidation of fire stations, and the number was soon reduced from 10 to 6 stations in Bay City.

View of Water Street looking south from Fremont, three days after the July 25, 1892 South End fire. One life was lost in Bay City's largest fire. Between 30 and 40 blocks of homes burned, and 1300 people left homeless. The fire covered an area east of the river to Jennison Street, between 28th and 34th. The conflagration began when sparks from a tugboat on the river ignited piles of lumber drying at Miller & Turner's Sawmill.

On April Fool's Day, 1940, the Ridotto Building at Madison and Center burned in a spectacular blaze. Firemen rescued 125 Business College students from upper floors. The Ridotto also housed a state liquor store and a well-known, third-floor ballroom.

The Fraser Hotel is seen here the day after a December 23, 1906 fire destroyed the hotel. It was so cold that December day that water from the firemen's hoses, despite the fire, quickly turned to ice. The building was replaced by the Wenonah Hotel in 1908. (See p. 69.)

First Hospitals Came Late to Bay City

While Saginaw had its first hospital, St. Mary's, in 1874, Bay City languished for another 25 years before decent hospital care arrived. Medical care facilities were extremely poor even during the boomtown years of the 1880s. Most illnesses and accidents—which were rampant in sawmill towns—were attended by local physicians in their homes. People who could not care for themselves or had a contagious illness were moved to the city "pest house" out in Hampton Township.

After St. Mary's met with success in East Saginaw as a subscription hospital—a $5 ticket purchased a mill worker or shanty boy treatment for one year—the Bay City Hospital opened in 1878 over a store at Fourth and Water streets. Though it advertised a modern "operating room," it appears that after opening several branches in Cheboygan, Marquette, and several Wisconsin cities, the hospital was more interested in selling tickets and franchises than in

The old Nathan B. Bradley house became the original home of Mercy Hospital in 1899. Bradley sold his three-story home to the Sisters of Mercy for $7,500. Located near the river at the foot of 14th Street, the hospital was enlarged several times. Mercy closed in the 1970s, and also housed, until 1964, the Bialy home and school for nurses.

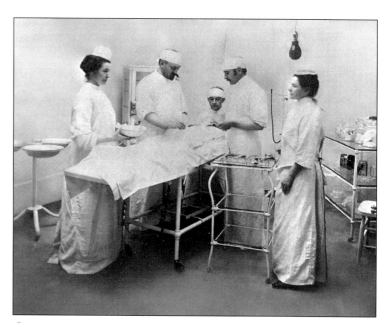

Operating room at Mercy Hospital c. 1911. Dr. Virgil Tupper is attending physician (at right). A new addition to Mercy in 1911 included an entire fourth-floor surgical area.

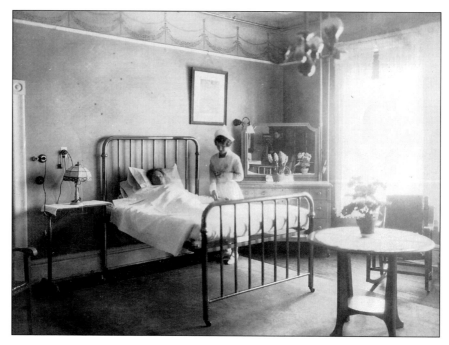

Typical hospital room, c. 1910. Mercy hospital eventually had a 335 bed capacity when a new addition was built after World War II. Many of the early rooms had "ensuite baths and utility rooms."

providing sound medical care. After a few years of moving around to several Bay City sites it disappeared from the city directories.

It was not until the post-lumber era, 1899, that the Sisters of Mercy arrived from Grand Rapids. They approached Bay City's authorities and were eventually offered the old Bradley home which the city purchased for $7,500. It was remodeled, equipped, and opened in 1900. Over the years Mercy Hospital grew to become a 333-bed facility.

Bay Medical Center, originally Bay City General, evolved from the original Detention Hospital for contagious diseases. It became a large, modern facility and by the 1970s, absorbed the now-closed Mercy Hospital. Two hospitals, the Bay City Lutheran Hospital and later the old West Bay City Hospital provided care to West Siders.

The Jones Clinic, enlarged to include the old Samaritan Hospital, was started in 1918 and located on 5th and Jackson streets. During the flu epidemic of 1918-19, black hearses were lined up on Jackson waiting for the victims who died in the new facility.

Staff of Bay City, West Side Hospital.

West Bay City Hospital

Bay County Infirmary in Hampton Township cared for contagious and venereal diseases. The County Board of Supervisors stands on the front porch of the facility in 1912.

PIONEER WOMEN HEALERS

Bay City's first medical doctor was a woman, Mrs. Elizabeth Wilcox Rogers. Originally settled in Portsmouth in 1837, she attended the sick and injured for the next 20 or so years. Mrs. Rogers was the daughter of a well-known Toronto physician under whom she studied medicine and apprenticed. She came to Portsmouth with her husband, a blacksmith, hired to work in Judge Albert Miller's original sawmill. As the only trained medical care worker in the pioneer settlement, Mrs. Rogers labored until 1850—when the first licensed physician arrived in Bay City—delivering babies, aiding the sick, and comforting the dying. She was remembered as the "ministering angel of the backwoods settlement."

Mrs. Roger's devotion was characteristic of yet another pioneer healer, Myra Parsons of Linwood. Mrs. Parsons—who left an account of her experiences in an extremely detailed diary—served as a healer and midwife in the last decades of the nineteenth century. At all hours of the day and night she writes about being called to deliver babies, tend to sick children, and amputate fingers, arms and legs of men injured in the mills. In November of 1888, she writes: "Charley Mank came to me and I went at once; at 4:45 A. M., a fine daughter was born to them, I engineered the entire campaign, came home at 6:30 A.M., went back at 10 A. M., and again at 7 P. M., and fixed mother and babe for the night." Myra Parsons had 7 children, tended the family's Linwood farm, and remained active in the community. She died at the young age of 41.

Mercy Hospital Ambulance, 1907.

Mrs. Elizabeth W. Rogers, pioneer settler, served as doctor and nurse to early settlers in Lower Saginaw from 1837 to 1850.

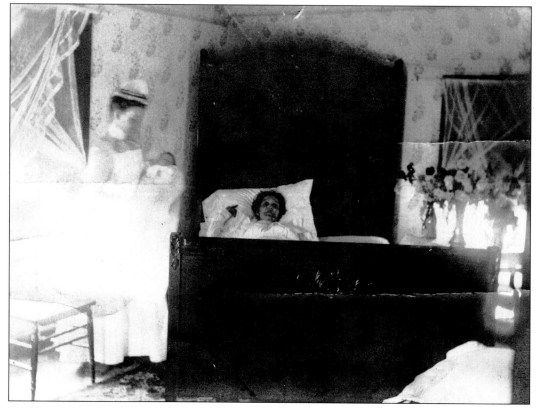

Home birth, c. 1900. Miss Brennan is holding new-born, Lucille, and mother Salome remains in bed.

LIBRARIES CAME SLOWLY TO BAY CITY

As a frontier town and one "not distinguished as a reading one," according to James G. Birney writing to Harriet Beecher Stowe in 1853, Bay City was slow to establish a public library system. Prior to the construction of public libraries, books were loaned through membership associations or lending organizations housed in public schools. In the 1868 city directory, W. H. DeLisle advertised a "Circulating Library" that loaned books for ten cents a week.

A library association was established in Bay City in 1869, but in 1874 the public schools used penal fines, $2,899, to purchase the association's books and start a free public library. This was housed in various sites around the city until the Main Library was opened on Center Avenue in 1922.

West Bay City actually had the first free public library. Henry Sage donated somewhere between $22,000 and $60,000—the actual costs remain unknown—in 1881 for construction of a library building, books, and a young men's debating school. The building on Midland Street, designed in a French Provencial style, was dedicated in 1884. Sage's benevolence did not come without a price. He proposed the public library in Wenona as early as 1871, but withheld the financial commitment until 1881 because he often believed he was met with "political hostility," and excessive taxes in West Bay City. His library was a promise drawn upon for ten years to attract favorable tax rulings in West Bay City.

The Bay City Public Library building on Center was based upon a gift of $35,000 from the Carnegie Corporation. Much of the work in securing the land and supplemental funding was done by pioneer industrialists William L. Clements, Henry B. Smith, C. R. Wells, and James E. Davidson. Andrew Carnegie built over 2800 libraries throughout the United States, and Bay City's is a replica of a fairly standard modified Georgian design widely used.

Henry W. Sage Library was a gift of lumberman Sage and opened in West Bay City in 1884.

Interior, children's reading room, at Bay City Public Library on Center Avenue between Monroe and Jackson streets.

The Bay City Public Library was built with funds from the Carnegie Foundation in 1922. The land was donated by several citizens of Bay City: H. B. Smith, C. R. Wells, James Davidson, and W. L. Clements.

BAY CITIANS IN THE CIVIL WAR

The State of Michigan was firmly behind Abraham Lincoln when the Civil War broke out in April of 1861. Even before actual hostilities began, the state organized two regiments of volunteers, and the Michigan Legislature refused to send delegates to early conferences that attempted reconciliation. Michigan eventually sent 87,000 men into the federal armies and of these 14,700 lost their lives.

In Bay City there was at first wide-spread support for the war. Volunteers were initially recruited in town by sheriff Benjamin F. Partridge as part of his 1st Michigan Lancers. Once the Lancers reported for duty they were asked to join other regiments, mainly the 16th Michigan. Partridge was commissioned as a first lieutenant. Each enlistee who was a family bread winner would receive $15 monthly pay.

The first volunteers from Bay City that went into service were men who enlisted with the 23rd Michigan Volunteer Infantry Regiment in East Saginaw in 1862. David Jerome, later a Governor of Michigan, was appointed head recruiting officer by Governor Austin Blair. Recruitment in Bay County was more difficult as the horrors of war became known and enlistments were of longer duration. The issue of slavery was hotly debated, and most men who joined the army did so to preserve the union rather than free the slaves.

Brig. Gen. Benjamin F. Partridge became Bay City's highest ranking Civil War officer, and as a lieutenant at Gettysburg, kept the Michigan men committed to battle during the desperate hand-to-hand fighting on Little Round Top.

Horace B. Mix was attached to Company C, U. S. Engineers. He was wounded at Vicksburg in 1863 and, after 11 months in the hospital, returned to service until the end of the war.

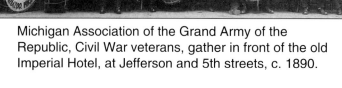

Michigan Association of the Grand Army of the Republic, Civil War veterans, gather in front of the old Imperial Hotel, at Jefferson and 5th streets, c. 1890.

Henry Landon, M. D. fought and was wounded at Fair Oaks as a member of Michigan's 7th Volunteers. Later he became an assistant surgeon for the regiment from 1863-64, and Bay City physician for many years after the war.

Capt. George Turner of Company B, 10th Michigan Volunteers, U. S. Engineers, was twice wounded at Stone River and later became Bay City's civil engineer.

THE 16TH MICHIGAN INFANTRY

Late in the war, Benjamin Partridge rose to the rank of General and was appointed commander of the 16th Michigan Infantry. Many Bay City volunteers were part of Partridge's company which eventually possessed one of the more distinguished war records. As part of the Army of the Potomac, the unit was in 38 major battles, including Bull Run, the Wilderness Campaign, Antietam, Cold Harbor, Petersburg, Fredericksburg, and others. At Gettysburg the 16th fought alongside the celebrated 20th Maine, commanded by Joshua Chamberlain, at Little Round Top. Historical records show that it was Lieutenant Partridge who kept the 16th Michigan from fleeing the battle field at Gettysburg. Out of ammunition, Partridge's men held, only with fixed bayonets, the last Confederate charge until fresh troops from New York led a counter attack that won the day for the Union Army. Partridge and the 16th continued fighting right until the end at Appomattox. At Appomattox, the regiment received 38 of the 71 battle flags captured during the final campaigns of the war.

Although his position in this group photo is unknown, this Civil War photograph reputedly was sent home to Bay City and includes resident James Manley.

The Grand Army of the Republic, Bay City Fife and Drum Crops and officers, c. 1890.

Legend Check

HENRY W. SAGE: INDUSTRIAL STATESMAN OR ROBBER BARON?

Henry W. Sage was the founder of the city of Wenona and a benefactor of West Bay City. A resident of Ithaca, New York, he built the company town around his large sawmill in 1864. Sage also donated around $43,500 for the construction of the Sage Library on the West Side. He ran one of the largest and most efficient sawmill operations in the entire country. Sage not only had investments in Bay City, but also in Ohio, Wisconsin, Canada, and several southern states. His mill was modern, fast, efficient and often used the latest in sawing technology. As an entrepreneur, Sage employed hundreds of men in Bay City and contributed significantly to town-building and the area's economy. In 1905 A. H. Gansser, in his pioneer history of Bay County, praised Sage as "one of the rich lumbermen who cared somewhat for posterity."

However, Sage's interests in West Bay City were foremost financial. He never lived there and his periodic visits to the mill town were obligatory functions, not affectionate or memorable undertakings. Sage wrote to his mill managers about "your people," "your streets," and "your town." West Bay City was just one tangential economic colony in his larger empire. Because he paid about 75 percent of the city's taxes, Sage successfully fought efforts to build sidewalks, sewers, and paved streets. In the 1870s he wrote to other absentee owners requesting their support in blocking these projects. His failure to modernize West Bay City is the main reason Bay City was reluctant to annex its cross-river neighbor until 1905. He had no real commitment—besides profit—to West Bay City and no responsibility to his employees.

Henry Sage, like many nineteenth-century industrialists, held strong social Darwinist beliefs that saw workers as less meritorious members of society. He housed them in several boardinghouses and a large tenement block that was later described as the "headquarters for rats, mice, cockroaches, bedbugs, and lice." Sage instructed his managers to "eject tenants that don't pay—uniformly—relaxing only in cases where there is sickness." In 1872 during a strike at his mill, Sage fired the entire workforce including his managers, and began to import Polish immigrants as strikebreakers. He was determined to let the "whole community feel the burden of the strike in their sense of folly."

As far as the Sage Library, this philanthropic act is tempered by the realization that Sage withheld 25 cents a week from his employees' pay to finance the library's reading room. In the 1880s, 25 cents was more than an hour's pay.

These practices alienated Bay Citians against the "money-grasping lumbermen." Though some of these practices were not out of place for the times, one can judge: Industrial Statesman or Robber Baron?

Lumberman Henry W. Sage

This is all that is left in West Bay City of the once massive Sage sawmill operations. The Sage company's main office building still stands at the western edge of Veterans Park and is today a private residence.

CHAPTER 5: LUMBERTOWN LEGACY

> *Think back for twenty years and see how many men you can remember who made their fortunes in Bay City and when they had made themselves independent, shook the dust off their feet and departed for some larger city. Were they of any benefit to Bay City? They made all they could and then looked up new fields and quietly departed.*
> *Bay City Tribune*, April 1, 1903, "His Majesty, B. F. J."

One lumbertown legacy that affected Bay City on all social, political, and economic levels was the significant number of absentee lumber barons who owned local sawmills. Several lumbermen who actually lived in Bay City emulated the absentee owners and, as the anonymous letter writer above indicated, when all the trees were gone, "shook the dust from their feet and departed for some larger city." Because they were not permanent residents, large operators seldom had the incentive to improve community life or raise their employees' wages. They exhausted the forests and subsequently abandoned their sawmills at the expense of workers and community. When they moved on they took with them the money, skills, and leadership necessary to rebuild Bay City economically and politically in the post-lumber era.

All of this created two separate and often distinct societies that have divided Bay City until this day. "Silk Stocking" resident and non-resident lumber barons created a social and economic climate where they often ignored and abdicated responsibilities to the community and its working-class citizens. "Blue collar" laborers came to distrust the city's economic leaders because they experienced job losses, wage cuts, and subsequent residential dislocations. To put some order and stability in their lives workers captured political control of Bay City and exerted leadership that was often narrow, parochial, and conservative.

The Michigan "cut-over." This "cowboy" from Bay City, rides through some of the millions of acres of stump-strewn lands left by the lumber barons in the 1890s. Clear-cutting, fires, and erosion left Michigan's forests underdeveloped and barren, often characterized today by large numbers of pulp trees.

The legacy of absentee ownership remained within the community a century later. A deep distrust of leadership persisted because leaders of the past seldom emphasized community building. Working-class politicians and unions created "machines" that labored primarily to perpetuate their existence. "White collar" economic leaders distrusted less-sophisticated elected officials, and the twain seldom met. Historic social divisions often prevented Bay City from developing a sense of common identity, purpose, and direction.

The "Lumbertown" left positive legacies as well. The working class that settled in Bay City developed strong ethnic neighborhoods that resonate with pride of home ownership, religious strength, persistence and remarkable endurance. Emanating from these neighborhoods were schools and churches that defined the lives of generations of Bay Citians.

A labor force, born of insecurity, forged a union movement that struggled for ample pay and secure employment in Bay City's industries. The workers eventually acquired a standard of living, financial security and opportunity that was unknown in the lumber era.

Some resident lumbermen set aside capital and built hardwood factories in the years immediately following the collapse of the pine industry. For a few years—after the turn of the century—several firms made Bay City an important center for the manufacture of hardwood flooring, veneer, plywood, woodenware, boxes, and "knock-down" wooden boats. While wood manufacturing was an expedient move for investors, it also kept the economy going during the post-lumber era adjustment period.

Economic and neighborhood stability provided nearby farmers with ready markets, and residents in town sometimes left work in the city to purchase farm land in the outlying townships of Bay County. For most of the twentieth century the durable economy maintained a viable downtown that did not experience the abandonment often associated with urban sprawl.

Lumbertown legacies remain in Bay City, some good and some not so good. Although change comes slowly to Bay City, changes have occurred, and the community will continue to be challenged by the legacies of the past into the next century.

As the residential areas spread out in Bay City and neighborhoods became more defined by income, house movings were common sights in the 1880s. Here a Queen Anne style home is moved into a fashionable residential block.

By 1900, Midland Street in West Bay City looked a good deal like it does today. Note Walsh's Grocery on the left and Fred Neumann, Justice of the Peace, and Jewell Stove and Range store.

The Lumber Barons

More than one half of Bay City's lumbermen were nonresident sawmill owners. This is a much larger percentage than existed in competing Michigan lumbertowns, and the figure is even more dramatic when one considers that two-thirds of Bay City's sawmill employees worked in several mammoth sawmills owned by outsiders. Since Bay City's absentee owners were the most powerful and wealthiest lumbermen, they often set the economic, social and cultural patterns that resident owners in Bay City followed.

Bay City was dependent on a regional network of lumber businesses that stretched south and eastward along the Great Lakes to upstate New York and from there east to towns on the Erie Canal. New Yorkers like Henry Sage and Thomas McGraw brought with them money and men who pioneered the logging business in Bay City. Business ties were often forged and new partners brought into local operations from regions beyond the Saginaw Valley. All of this makes it clear that it was very difficult—despite the rags to riches myth—for the independent, self-made man to achieve his fortune in Bay City.

Recent studies of the social origins of 223 lumbermen from Bay City, Saginaw, and Muskegon—the leading lumbertowns in nineteenth-century Michigan—found that in Bay City nearly 75 percent of the lumbermen were born in the United States (Most of the foreign-born came from Great Britain.). Nearly 75 percent came from middle- or upper-class backgrounds; and some 56 percent of the millowners had prior experience somewhere else in the lumber business. Likewise they were better educated than the norm: a solid core, 55 percent, had more than a common-school education. Eighty-five percent of Bay City's lumbermen were members of the Republican party; and almost all were Protestant —especially Presbyterians, Episcopalians, or Congregationalists. So the typical lumber mill owner in Bay City did not live there and was not a "poor boy made good," or an escapee from European poverty. They came from family-run businesses in New York and frequently shared common culture and background.

The wealth of Bay City's resident lumber barons was most apparent in the residential district along Center Avenue. Splendid mansions—large and often three stories tall—marked not only where lumber-

continued on page 90

S.O. Fisher's residence in West Bay City (1898) was located at 205 N. Mountain. Fisher acquired his wealth through lumber (camps in Pinconning and Fisherville), electric streetcars, and real estate development.

Lumberman, Congressman, and real estate promoter, S. O. Fisher.

Children from the neighborhood gather in front of Judge Wright's house at 9th and Sherman streets.

Photograph of the Madison Avenue Methodist Church parsonage in 1901. The home was bulit in 1897. On the veranda are the Rev. Dwight L. Ramsdell, his wife and baby, and mother and sister. Their sons are on the sidewalk and on the left is the church Sexton, Mr. Sterling.

men lived but also where other successful entrepreneurs built their homes. Some ornate houses were gifts given by the barons to their daughters upon marriage. The largest houses on Center had third-floor ballrooms and enough bedrooms to accommodate a score of overnight guests. Often taking up the entire block—homes like William McEwan's or A. E. Bousfield's (the Colonial Apartments building) sat away from the street and were commonly fenced in with uniquely designed picket or wrought-iron fences.

Social functions also separated the classes. The Eddys, McEwans, Bousfield, and others, when they were not traveling around visiting their forest lands and cutting operations, took their family and guests to the Wood's Opera House, East Saginaw's Music Academy, and frequently to other mansions for dinner parties. Avid sportsmen like Arnold Boutell along with several Saginaw lumbermen built the Tobico Hunting Club as a private hunting and fishing preserve.

Philanthrophy, while not practiced extensively in Bay City, was another endeavor that distinguished some lumbermen from others. Alex Folsom built a church and the Y.M.C.A., James I. Fraser donated money for the First Baptist Church building, and Henry Sage constructed the library and gave land for several West Side churches.

In the early years Bay City lumbermen were also active in local politics. Nathan B. Bradley was the first mayor of Bay City in 1865 and later served as state senator and U. S. Congressman. Other pioneers—W. C. Fay and J. J. McCormick—also held public office in the early seventies; however after that few lumbermen held positions of prominence in Bay City. The lumber barons did not concentrate exclusively on Bay City politics because they were often owners of widespread timber lands or were absentee owners.

A caricature of C. C. Whitney, druggist and owner of Pomroy & Whitney, manufacturer of crackers and biscuits, came from Adrian and later Alpena to build his varied business interest in Bay City. The drawing was part of a 1905 listing of 33 prominent Bay Citians done by Newspaper cartoonists of Michigan.

Whitney's residence, photographed in 1912, still stands at the corner of Center Avenue and Lincoln

Residence of William McEwan, 702 Center Avenue. McEwan, and his brother, John, came to Bay City in 1851 and started in the sawmill business. They developed extensive logging operations in what is today downtown Clare, MI. McEwan Street in Clare is named after Bay City's McEwans.

L. E. Noyes' Bay City home, c. 1888. Noyes arrived in Bay City in 1869 and engaged in the buying and selling of logs and lumber. He essentially was a lumber merchant and centered his vast trading network in Bay City.

The Charles B. Curtiss residence 924 Center Avenue. Curtiss owned the Bay City Dredge Company and he built this home, which remained in the family for decades, in 1891.

Lumbertown Laborers

"The sawmill men are a cog in a vast machine."
A Bay City attorney in *Detroit Labor Leaf*, July 22, 1885

The prosperous years of the lumber boom in Michigan rolled right along into the mid 1880s. Everyone, especially the lumber barons and the lumbertown businessmen, profited within this new industrial order: everyone, that is except the common workingman. Sawmill workers, shipbuilders, and wood-workers all saw the lumbermen-capitalists in Bay City make repeated attempts to bring order, economy, and stability to a labor force that was having difficulty adapting to the new industrial order. Logging railroads, new machines, faster saws, longer hours, declining wages, and competition from immigrants all pressed upon the workers. The number of skilled wood workers dwindled, and craftsmen often became just other factory hands. The leisurely work pace, common in earlier, small, family-run mills, also disappeared. Steam and electric power intensified and regimented the work routine.

Men were driven by foremen—often hired by far-away absentee owners—who bragged about new production records set in their sawmills. "The sawmill men are part of their machines," a Bay City attorney wrote in 1885. "They could not even stop for a drink of water but must keep up the labor just as the inanimate machinery. The men are a cog in a vast machine." Many sawmill workers fed flesh and bone to the steel blades that at times ran twenty-four hours a day. A millman or shingle worker was easily recognized on the streets of Bay City by his misshapen hands or missing fingers. Shipbuilders at the West Side yards found their ears ringing incessantly from the noise of pounding rivets in new, steel-hulled ships. Deafness was often their only escape. Carpenters in barrel, box, or flooring plants came out at night coughing and spitting oak, maple or walnut dust. Asthma, breathing problems and stomach disorders

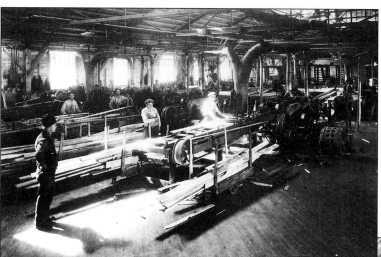

The Kneeland-Bigelow hardwood plant, on Water St. between 19th and 21st streets, manufactured hardwood products well into the 20th century. Here a supervisor oversees workers mass-producing hard wood flooring on new machines.

Child labor was common in the sawmills prior to the turn of the century. Note the number of young boys working in this Middlegrounds sawmill and the boy on the log without shoes.

were endemic in the sawmill towns. There were no hospitals in Bay City and no accident insurance or compensation to provide for the injured or their families. A few lumbermen offered gifts of money, but in most cases the maimed and debilitated adapted, recovered, and out of necessity, soon went back to work.

Most of the workers arriving in Bay City in the 1870s and 1880s came from three groups: (1) local, native-born farmers and their families and some itinerant Irish; (2) immigrants from Canada, and Germany; and (3) later arriving immigrants from Poland, Sweden, and the Lowlands. Since the sawing season lasted only six months, it was difficult to keep a permanent labor force in town. Native-born workers and the Germans were often considered the most reliable. French-Canadians often disliked work in the sawmills and remained extremely transient. When labor unrest first hit Bay City in 1872, Sage, McGraw, and others began to import Poles as strikebreakers to work in their sawmills. This practice continued into the 1880s, and caused resentment toward the Poles by mill workers who saw them as scab laborers willing to work for lower wages. While the French-Canadians (41%), Germans (21%), and Poles (12%) were the largest ethnic blocs in Bay City in 1890, the English (7%), Irish (5%), Lowlanders from Belgium and Holland (4%), and Swedes (2%) made up other elements of the large, foreign-born population. African-Americans and Native Americans made up less than one percent.

The large number of transient workers made for a relatively poor working-class population, and almost all immigrant laborers earned wages below the average city wage. In the sawmills daily wages ranged from $1.30 for a common laborer to $1.60 for a semi-skilled hand. The work day usually began at 5:45 or 6:00 A. M. and ran until 8:45 when a morning break occurred to replace and sharpen dulled saw blades. The men resumed work from 9:00 until noon when they had a half-hour lunch break. Another blade replacement break came at 3:00, and the mill shut down at 6:00 or 6:15 P. M.

Immigrant women and children also entered the

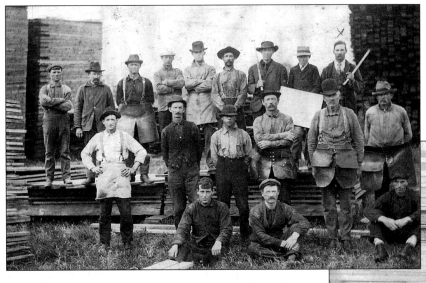

Sawmill workers stacking boards to dry at the Vance lumberyard, 1890. Injuries were common in the sawmills. The worker on the far left (in white apron) appears to have a finger missing on his right hand.

Workers at Bay City's shipyards often suffered loss of hearing as a result of years of pounding rivets inside steel hulls.

Because of working conditions and pay, Bay City became one of the state's most unionized cities. Here the Sheet Metal Workers Union posed in front of the post office prior to a labor day parade.

work force in large numbers. This enabled families to pool resources in order to buy a home or simply to survive. In Bay City women laborers received about 80 cents a day on average, while children were paid 50 cents per day. Children and women cut employers' expenses in half and were thus attractive alternatives to hiring male workers. Young boys could be seen working in sawmills and shingle mills, and young girls labored especially in Bay City's knitting mills. Boys went to work at 12; however, more girls remained in school after that age than boys.

Although the workday was long and arduous, some immigrant families found life in the mills rewarding. A very large percentage of German and Polish workers built their own homes from cheap and scrap lumber available around the mills. By 1885, these two groups, especially, had planted their feet firmly on the lower rungs of the occupational ladder in Bay City. It is not surprising, therefore, that when the lumbermen began to cut wages in the sawmills, Poles and Germans became the backbone of the largest labor protest movement in nineteenth-century Michigan.

Child laborers, whether in agriculture or industrial jobs, averaged about 50 cents per day. Note the young boy in front with a pipe in his mouth.

It was not uncommon to find children working in sawmills at ten years of age. Few boys went to school after 12. This photo is taken at the Hall mill in Essexville.

THE "TEN HOURS OR NO SAWDUST" STRIKE OF 1885.

It has frequently been written that the the "Ten Hours or No Sawdust" strike that began in Bay City on July 6, 1885 was a victory for the workers against the predatory practices of the lumber barons. Nothing could be further from the truth.

Agitation for strike action began in Bay City in the spring of 1885 when a drop in the price of lumber prompted lumbermen to cut the average wage from $1.98 to $1.77 per day. While the men reluctantly accepted the lower pay, they began to demand a 10-hour workday instead of the old 12-hour day. When the lumber barons in Bay City, many of them absentee owners, refused to consider the shorter hours, laborers left the sawmills on July 6, and roamed the waterfront of the city closing down all the sawmills. As they marched through the streets, fights broke out with workers reluctant to leave the sawmills. In the next several days Bay City's mill workers moved upriver and shut down all the mills along both sides of the river in Saginaw.

In Bay City, on July 9, a large rally of 2,000 men was held at Madison Park. It was reported by the sheriff that the leaders were mostly "Polanders" and some Germans. The men demanded 10-hour workdays and old wages. Because so many lumbermen were nonresidents, local businessmen in town backed the strikers. They extended credit at their stores to out-of work-millhands, and newspapers editorialized in favor of the strike. The mayor and local authorities also sympathized with the workers.

Minor episodes of violence prompted Governor Russell Alger, a wealthy lumberman and investor in a Saginaw mill, to send the state militia to the valley. On July 14, Alger arrived in Bay City himself and addressed a crowd of workers from the steps of the Fraser Hotel. He blamed the strike on its leaders and told the workers to go back to work. Alger distrusted all immigrants and saw them as "bad people," easily led by their more-cunning spokesmen. He blamed immigrant Poles and Germans for the strike. Alger was partly right. Because they were usually the lowest paid and did the hardest work, the Poles and others—even a number of black workers—became the backbone of the strike.

After the Governor called in the militia even the Knights of Labor, who organized the strike after it began, encouraged the workers to return to work. When skilled hands in Saginaw began to go back to the mills, Bay City lumbermen sent their logs upriver to be cut. Resistance in Bay City weakened by early September especially as workers realized they needed some income before the mills shut for the season. Gradually they returned to work in the Bay City sawmills. Most went back at 11 or 12 hours with the original reduction in pay. The strike was a failure.

In Bay City there were too many men, too many logs, too many mills, and too many machines for the workers to be successful. They could not overcome the power of the lumber barons. Any prolonged strike action in Bay City would have inevitably resulted in many mills closing for good—as Sage had threatened to do at his sawmill. Lumbermen had little regard for the long-term well-being of Bay City or its workers. Absentee owners caused local business people considerable distress by their willingness to keep the mills closed for 60 days. Small businessmen saw little sense of community responsibility being exercised by the lumbermen.

Ethnic groups became further alienated from the lumbermen and the community. They used their status as laborers to effect some political control, and they eventually developed strong ethnic neighborhoods where immigrant workers shared experiences and found refuge from unemployment, poverty, and the pitfalls of the new industrial life. "Progress"—the American Dream—was reflected in local social and political organizations; not city-wide promotion or social and economic integration. The strike was the turning point of Bay City's history; it exposed a split in the community that was to last for more than a century.

Governor Russell A. Alger called the State Militia to Bay City.

Bay City Mayor George H. Shearer sympathized with the strikers.

Representative Thomas Barry, strike leader.

Ethnic Neighborhoods

The strike of 1885 certainly revealed that the people of Bay City were not bound together by any one culture. It became clear that they were most commonly separated from one another by economics, neighborhoods, culture, language, and religion. Immigrants into Bay City were caught in a paradox of being recruited and welcomed as cheap laborers, but being looked down upon and ostracized by the better classes. Caught up in nineteenth-century social Darwinism, the lumbermen and their associates saw working-class immigrants as innately shiftless, less-capable members of society. Their relationships with their workers were strictly economic. By the decade of the strike, 44% of Bay City's population was foreign born; mostly French-Canadians, Germans, and Poles. (This was a larger percentage than even in some other well-known immigrant cities like Detroit's 39% foreign-born, and Milwaukee's 40%.)

An example of the homes built by workers in Bay City's ethnic neighborhoods. This house is in the French populated Banks area and still stands at 500 Transit Street.

This Queen Anne style home was popular as an upper middle-class residence. Note the wooden sidewalks, twig chairs on the porch, and three different bike styles in turn-of-the-century Bay City.

The John Guillett homestead in 1876, at 816 Nebobish Avenue, is a good example of middle-class and successful working-class lifestyle.

It is, therefore, not surprising that newcomers would quickly establish their own neighborhoods, churches, schools, businesses, and social societies. Here they found mutual support and were able to accommodate the discrimination sometimes evident in the industrial lumbertown. The family home and neighborhood in Bay City became the center of life. Crowded together on small lots, these one- or two-story homes were close to the sidewalks and streets. Houses all had front porches and "front rooms" where the residents could keep watch and be part of the neighborhood. They did not erect barriers to neighborliness and ethnic identity. Though their houses were often made of scrap lumber, they were frequently painted in bright colors and kept neat and clean. Nearby businesses reflected the ethnic community: Polish and German meat markets and bakeries; Jewish delicatessens; and Irish pubs. The ethnic neighborhoods in Bay City stood out as places where the homeowner could pass his life in work, comfort, and relative contentment.

For many immigrant families in Bay City hard work brought reasonable success. Here members of the Kowalski family sit proudly in their new touring car at S. Henry and E. Jenny streets in 1906.

One German neighborhood in Bay City centered in Salzburg on the West Side. This view, from the roof of Putz's Hardware, looks north down Wenona. In the center of photo is the office for Kantzler's lumberyard, today the Wanigan deli.

The French Canadians

French-speaking Canadians were the earliest settlers in Bay City. Few Frenchmen came directly from France, but were transient workers many coming from Quebec and Maine where they were woodsmen, or employees in the early cotton mills of New England. Some engaged in the fur trade, but most became fishermen and sawmill workers. They continued to live along the river at the mouth of the Saginaw in Banks, Frenchtown, and Essexville. In a sample residential block along Campbell Street between Dolsen and Belinda in the 1880 census, French-speakiing Canadians made up 88% of the residents.

Some French-Canadians were recruited to work as boom men during the 1885 strike. Census data for Bay City indicates a definite transient pattern for many French arrivals. Over a 25 year period in the last quarter of the century, few French stayed around in Bay City for long periods of time. They reputedly did not al-

The Cartier brothers were early French settlers in Pinconning and Bay City. The three brothers (center and back) are Noah, Basitlus, and Joseph.

The St. Laurent's Bros.' original peanut house was located at First and Water streets when it opened in 1904. In 1917 they moved to their present location at Third and Water.

Joseph Primeau's grocery store on Johnson Street. Mr. Primeau is on the far right and is an example of those French settlers that remained in town and built small businesses within their ethnic neighborhoods.

ways adjust comfortably to life in the sawmills. They preferred to work in the woods or on the waters. Considering their work and transience, the French populations in Bay City were predominantly young and male. Women often worked at a young age outside the home and children did not attend school as long as other immigrant children in town.

As residents, those that did not work in the mills or as fishermen, established small businesses in Banks. The French were somewhat clannish in Banks and Frenchtown. They married within neighborhood ethnic boundaries and established the first Catholic Church in the area, St. Joseph's in 1850, on Washington near the present-day post office. The dramatic increase of French workers in the late nineteenth century led to the creation of Visitation parish by 450 families in 1895. They also established a Catholic parish in Linwood, St. Anne's church. Once the sawmills closed the French turned to fishing as an occupational mainstay in Bay City.

The Dolsen School in 1883 was located near the French neighborhoods, and a good many of its students were children of nearby French merchants and workers.

The Ingers and LaRoche meat market was located in the "Frenchtown" neighborhood on the corner of Woodside and Belinda streets.

The Poles

The Polish who settled in Bay City came from a politically divided homeland where few peasants could acquire property. Many Poles had been shifted around by a century of political change in Poland and remained landless migrants before departing for America. The Poles who came to Bay City originally left from Prussian Poland or Poznania and they came as agricultural laborers to work some of the farms owned by Germans. In Poland, German landlords often saw the Poles as indolent and cunning because they tried to escape work on German-owned Polish farms. These attitudes were transferred to the Saginaw Valley. Near Alpena a group of Polish farm hands killed an oppressive German landlord. Many Polish men, women and children worked as laborers in the fields hoping to save, like the Germans, to buy a farm.

When McGraw's mammoth sawmill burned down in 1872 and was replaced by an even larger complex, McGraw hired a recent Polish immigrant, Ludwig Danielewski (Daniels), as an agent to recruit Poles to work in the new mill. During the depression years of 1873-74, other mill owners in Bay City—like Henry Sage—hired Poles as strikebreakers because they worked at reduced wages. As sawmill workers the Poles were often given, as one contemporary noted, "the lowest grade of work." The hiring of Polish strikebreakers alienated the community against not only the lumbermen, but also Polish, "scabs." In time, however, subjected to low pay, layoffs, and wage cuts they joined with other immigrant workers and formed a strong labor movement to protect their interests.

Joseph Scubeck ran a grocery store in the Polish neighborhood at Broadway and 30th streets. Here Mr. Scubeck holds a display of cigars and pipes. Smoking a cigar was a pleasure many working-class Polish men (and boys) enjoyed after work.

The Kaczynski family, c. 1915. Polish immigrants Josephine and Frank, (seated), and children, spouses, and assorted grandchildren attest, in this photo, to the reality of the extended Polish family in south Bay City.

Because of their labor difficulties both on the farm and the factory, "the Poles occupied the outlying districts of Bay City—from 14th Street southward— and were content to leave the rest of the citizenry alone." Here they organized around Polish churches, like St. Stanislaus established in 1874, and created brotherhood and fraternal organizations that preserved their culture and elements of life they held dear —family, farm or neighborhood, and household.

Their European experience and ethnic prejudice explains why the Poles were slow to relinquish the speech and customs of their homeland. They also did not—like the Germans—see immigration as an opportunity for upward mobility. They wanted the simple life—the Polish community—that they could not have had in Poland. They found that life style in Bay City and nourished it around their many Catholic churches (St. Stanislaus, St. Hyacinth's, in the South End, St. Hedwig's, and St. Valentine's on the West Side, and St. Anthony of Padua in Fisherville), their own businesses, newspapers—the *Polski Sztandar* —, Pulaski Hall, and their neighborhoods. In these neighborhoods they owned their homes almost as frequently as the German settlers, and valued education especially in their Catholic schools. Owning a home was one of the surest ways of achieving upward mobility for the Polish.

Ludwig Danielewski (Daniels), a tailor by trade, came to Bay City in 1867 and was active in recruiting new Polish immigrants to work in the city's South End sawmills in the 1870s.

The Pawlaczyk family came to Bay City in 1903. A second wave of Polish settlers came to Bay City to work in the coal mines and beet fields after the turn of the century. Micharlene and Joseph are seated in front with children Andrew, Kate, Mary, Joseph, Casimer, Julia, and Robert, in front.

A large number of Polish workers were recruited from Pennsylvania, Ohio, and West Virginia to work in the newly opened Bay City coal mines between 1900 and 1910.

The Germans

The German settlers who came to the bay area had, as one letter-writer noted "an eye for the soil." They had an "uncanny" ability to select good farmland, and many intended to remain in Bay City just long enough to earn money and buy land outside the city. After the Civil War, new arrivals, though, came with insufficient funds to purchase land in the county. Subsequently, the Germans who continued to emigrate settled in the city and readily found jobs in the sawmills.

The state of Michigan hired a Saginaw resident, Max Allardt, as the first and only Commissioner of Emigration. He set up an office in Hamburg, Germany and, between 1869 and 1874, heavily recruited thousands of Germans to come to Michigan and the Saginaw Valley especially. German immigrants who had little money were encouraged, as a state immigration officer wrote, ". . . to give up such preposterous ideas as farming, and look out for work in the cities among the lumbermen."

Germans flocked into Salzburg, which was about 66% German in 1880, and later into West Bay City.

The German Staudacher family lived at 910 Salzburg Avenue. Long-time residents they were mill workers and farmers. Pictured are parents Rosina and Frederick with Lydia, Ethel, and Walter.

The Salzburg German band posing on Midland Street. The band was well-known for years and played at Lutheran church functions, parades, and other celebrations.

William and Alvinia Schnettler's wedding carriages, 1910. Left to right, Fred Peters and Emma Zube; Charles Zube and Lena DuRussell; William Zube and Hulda Pett; and bride and groom.

Portsmouth, across the river, and an area along Lincoln between 10th and 14th streets, also attracted German settlers. Germans were ideal workers because they were "industrious, religious, often educated, and fairly easily assimilated." They came to Bay City as family units, and more Germans owned their own homes than any other group in Bay City, native- or foreign-born. Also the Germans moved up the occupational ladder more quickly than others and acquired employment as engineers or foremen in the sawmills. Their children frequently went to school and fewer German women worked outside of the home.

The great majority of the Germans were Lutherans who established numerous churches after the initial founding of St. Paul's in Frankenlust. German Catholics built St. Boniface church on the East Side in 1874, and in 1894 a mission church was started along Ionia Avenue in Salzburg. This mission church became Holy Trinity parish. German immigrants were joiners, and, in addition to church life, they formed several social clubs like *Arbeiter Unterstuetzing* and built the large Arbeiter Hall at Johnson and Seventh streets.

Henry Kramer and Family. Born in Prussia in 1827, Henry came to Bay City in 1847 and later brought his wife, Fredericka, from Brunswick. They later lived in Monitor township.

German Arbeiter Hall was a commodious building located on two acres at Johnson and Seventh streets.

A good example of a successful German-owned business was Burkhardt's meat market located at 306 Salzburg. "Inspected" meats and fresh game were featured, when in season.

Wedding photographs like this were common at the turn-of the-century ethnic celebrations. This is the wedding of William and Alvinia Schnettler, September 9, 1910. The house still stands at the corner of Finn and German roads near Munger.

The Swedish

Swedish immigrants into Michigan frequently followed the "Cousin Jack" principle of migration. Informal channels of communication—letters and word-of-mouth—to the old country alerted friends and relatives of the opportunities in Michigan. Many Swedes were contract laborers who came over to work on logging crews where they were reputedly "unexcelled" as lumberjacks. After the logging drive each spring many came into Bay City for seasonal and permanent employment in West Side sawmills. Initially the Swedish settlers were predominantly male, but many families soon followed.

The earliest Swedish immigrants arrived in the 1870s; by 1880 sufficient numbers had settled in West Bay City that a congregation of 50 organized the Swedish Evangelical Lutheran Sion Church (Messiah Lutheran) on Catherine Street. A year later Henry Sage donated land on Henry Street for a parsonage. Eventually the Evangelical Free Church, and the Swedish Baptist church on East Jenny were also built. A small number of Swedes also settled on the East Side along Cass and Marsac streets.

Early Swedish settlers to Bay City: The Nelson family, father Neal and mother Benkta were both born in Sweden. Children (in back row) Charles, Art, Harry, and Christine. In front, Ede and Emma.

The original Messiah Lutheran Church, c. 1895. The church was built in the Swedish neighborhood along Henry and Jenny streets in 1881 on land donated by Henry Sage. (See also the Johnson family store, p. 139.)

Confirmation class of the Swedish Lutheran Sion Church (Messiah), c. 1888. Seated in center is Pastor Peter Lofgren who came to West Bay City in 1883 and built the first parish school house on Henry Street.

The Belgians and Dutch

"First the fish—then the sawmills—then the farms. The French followed the sawmills, the Dutch developed the farms." While not completely accurate, this pioneer summary does explain in part the Belgian and Dutch settlements in the Essexville-Hampton Township area. Many of the early Dutch and Belgian settlers began to arrive in the 1850s and 1860s. Their numbers increased as others wrote back home about the farming prospects in Hampton Township. In 1873 twelve families arrived together aboard the *S. S. Maas* from Holland and purchased land in and around Essexville.

The Belgians arrived in the same time period, and because they were experienced sugar-beet growers they began to plant beets in the cut-over lands east of town. Many of these early Belgian and Dutch residents also came in part because the first Catholic missionary priests in Lower Saginaw attending to the French were Belgian (Fr. Joseph Kindekins) or Dutch (Fr. H. T. H. Schutjes). In 1884 the Dutch and Belgians built St. John the Evangelist Catholic Church on the corner of Pine and Hudson streets. The first priest, Fr. Cornelius Roche, soon built a rectory and Holy Rosary Academy for young girls. When the sugar beet industry prospered shortly after the turn of the century, a good many more Belgian and Dutch settlers came to the area as farm laborers. St. John's numbered 2,000 parishioners in 1900.

Frank VanMullekom came from Holland in 1888 and settled on Borton Road. He dug ditches until 1917, and was so efficient at it that he was well known as the "Human Dredge."

St John's Church and school in the background located on Pine and Hudson streets.

St. John the Evangelist Catholic Church and School were the center of Dutch and Belgian religious activity. Here several boys pose at St. John's school after a play rehearsal in 1904.

The Irish

Despite the state-wide reputation of Bay City's annual St. Patrick's Day parade, the number of actual Irish settlers was small in comparison to other immigrant groups that settled in town. Around 1890 foreign-born Irish made up around five percent of the population. However, many who told the census-taker that they were born in Canada or Great Britain could well have been of Irish descent.

The Irish began to trickle into the Saginaw Valley as laborers on the early canals and railroads in the 1850s and 1860s. While famine and hardships in Ireland spurred immigration, many Irish came to Michigan via Canada. They found work in the lumbering industry and a good many lived and worked for the Michigan Central Railroad on the West Side. Strong in their Catholicism, the English-speaking Irish centered around St. James parish between Monroe and Farragut south of Columbus to 14th streets. On the West Side the majority of the parishioners at St. Mary's, established in 1873, were Irish. The St. Patrick's Day parade began in 1955 and has grown to what some claim "is the greatest St. Pat's parade this side of New York City."

As part of a school music program at St. James school in 1933, John G. Young and Kathleen Battle Leikert remember traditional Irish immigrant customs brought to America.

St James Catholic Church was established in the late 1860s and the Catholic High school was the oldest coed institution in the country dating back to 1873.

The St. Patrick's Day parade is an annual celebration that began in 1955 and, despite the weather, is held every March. It has grown to become one of the largest St. Patrick's Day celebrations in the country. This photo is of the 1958 parade along Center Avenue.

Jewish Settlers

The earliest Jewish immigrants arrived in the 1870s mostly from Germany, Russia, and Poland. However even before 1872, when the first Jewish organization of B'nai B'rith was organized in Bay City, other Jewish merchants, peddlers, and clothiers had arrived in the lumbertown from France and Hungary. A substantial number of the earlier families also came from the Kurland region of Latvia. There were Jewish-owned drygoods stores, run by Leopold Ehrlich and by A. and I. Grabowsky, as well as two Jewish-run clothing stores in 1870. These men were among the twenty-five who signed the first B'nai B'rith charter.

In 1882, the Shaarey-Zedek Orthodox Congregation was formed by 11 members who withdrew from the original temple. For a long time there were three separate congregations in Bay City, the Anshe Chesed (B'nai-B'rith) or reformed temple on Adams, the Shaarey-Zedek located on North Van Buren and Eleventh streets, and the Temple of Abraham at Jackson and 10th streets. Jewish people lived north of Columbus between Madison and Farragut streets. They frequently operated downtown department, clothing and jewelry stores. Several Columbus area stores were also owned by members of the Jewish community. In 1960 Temple Israel, designed by Alden Dow, was built at the corner of Center Avenue and Green, and today serves the city's combined Jewish community.

Temple of Abraham, 254 N. Jackson Street was erected in 1915. The Jewish community in Bay City traces its roots back to the early 1870s, and the first congregation worshiped along the river in the McEwan building between 4th and 5th streets.

In 1960, the combined Jewish communities in Bay City built Temple Israel on the corner of Center Avenue and Green. The temple was designed by Midland architect, Alden Dow.

Kahn's Jewelry and Music store is an example of one of the several businesses established by Jewish pioneers to Bay City. Alex Kahn stands in the doorway of his store at 814 Water Street.

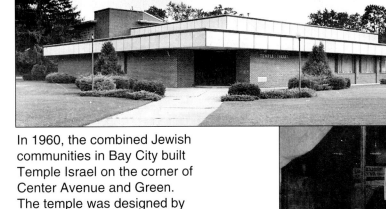

The African-Americans

Lured by newspaper advertisements for sawmill laborers, the railroads, and opportunities for success in the lumbertowns, some blacks came to Bay City seeking employment and their fortunes. Numbers were never large in the last century: there were approximately 200 blacks in Bay City in 1880. Some of the early African-American settlers were escaped slaves who came along the underground railway into Bay City while others came from Ohio and New England.

Blacks were employed as barbers, hotel waiters, cooks, and on the early railroads in Bay City. Several self employed teamsters, like Daniel Fairfax in Bay City, and restaurant owner, James H. Baker, achieved financial success. Baker's son, Oscar W. Baker, later became the city's first African-American attorney.

About a third of black residents were employed in the sawmills. Most worked as firemen (workers who tended the giant steam boilers in the mills), and as salt-boilers and salt-packers. Few African-Americans worked in the woods during the winter months.

In West Bay City a boardinghouse owned by Andrew Bird, within Sage's sawmill grounds, housed black workers. A good many black families arrived in Bay City and working wives were commonly employed as domestics in town. Much of the early black community attended the Second Baptist Church on Monroe and Tenth streets. When the sawmills closed in the 1890s, and the job market became smaller, a good many blacks were pressured out of service jobs by whites and departed the city.

A second migration from the South began during both wars as industrial jobs opened in the city.

Aunt Kate Brooks owned and operated a stand that sold sundry items on Fifth Street in 1885.

Bay City's first African-American attorney, Oscar W. Baker began practice in 1902. His father owned a Bay City restaurant for years in the lumber era.

Because the population was not large, there was little discrimination against blacks in Bay City in the late nineteenth century. Several families did well and were able to send their children to high school, where they participated in school activities rather than work.

HISPANIC SETTLERS

The demand for seasonal harvest workers in the sugar-beet fields prompted Mexican migrants to come north in the first decades of the twentieth century. Many came as transient laborers and stayed only a short while. In time, realizing the potential for free schooling and more stable employment, a significant Mexican-American community began to settle in Bay City. In time Mexican workers found jobs in the sugar-beet processing plants and some of the heavy industries in the Saginaw Valley. A second wave of migrants took root in Bay City in the 1940s and 1950s.

Our Lady of Guadalupe Chapel and Community Center, on Broadway in south Bay City, serves as a center for Mexican Americans and the migrant families who continue to follow the annual harvest. Additional Hispanic families arrived to work at General Motors in the 1960s, and while some live along south Broadway, most of the 3,500 or so Mexican-American families are scattered throughout the city.

The Guadalupe Center Church and Community Center on Broadway functions not only as a community center for Bay City's Hispanic people, but is an active outreach center in the summer months aiding migrant laborers in Bay County.

A novena to Our Lady of Guadalupe is celebrated every December at the South End church. The Danza dance is part of this celebration. The young ladies are carrying incense.

Our Lady of Guadalupe Church's first communion class in 1990.

Agriculture

In 1874 the number of farms in Bay County was listed as 531; by 1880 there were nearly 1,000 farms. Once the land was cleared of its trees many city residents left to take up farming in the county. By 1935, there were 3,391 farms in Bay County. Although there has been a steady decline since then, the farms have increased in size, and Bay County remains a "garden spot of Michigan."

Growing and processing sugar beets in Bay County was a venture enthusiastically received by many farmers. Sugar beets were first imported from Germany and grown in Hampton Township in 1896. The state offered a bounty in 1897 of one cent per pound for all sugar manufactured in Michigan. This was an effort to reclaim cut-over land and encourage investment in agriculture to replace lumbering. Bay City quickly built three processing plants. However, the industry over built, and Eastern sugar-trust competition forced most of the plants out of business by 1904. Small companies later merged and formed Bay City's large Monitor Sugar Company.

Farmers also grew chicory, which was dried and ground into a powder to use as a substitute for coffee. Frugality, persistence, and hard work on the part of Bay County's Dutch, German, and Polish farmers brought prosperity to several small, rural agricultural settlements around Bay City.

The John H. Sharp family of Essexville. Although Sharp was primarily a fisherman by trade his home in rural Essexville is an excellent representation of a pioneer family residence.

Horses on display at Boutell farm in Hampton Township, c. 1902. Ira Sagle holds the black horses and Bill Zimmerman is between the four white animals. Zimmerman worked the farm as a hand for seven years. The barn itself is a magnificent structure with three floors and intricate decoration. A. Miller, the barn builder stands at far left.

Immigrant women and children, and some men, hired on as farm hands especially during the fall beet-sugar harvest. Here Polish laborers are weeding sugar beets on the Boutell farm, c. 1900.

MYRA PARSONS: PIONEER!

Recent literature and popular television dramas that picture the accomplished woman pioneer achieving a great deal against substantial odds are not fiction. Bay County had its own "medicine woman" and frontier heroine in Myra Parsons of Linwood.

A major treasure in the Bay County Historical Museum is the diary of Myra describing most of her life in Linwood from 1877 to 1892. Not only did she record the details of running the family farm along side of her husband, Mahlon Edwin Parsons, but she also gave birth to seven children, tended to the medical needs of the nearby sawmill workers and farm families, and found time to become a leader in the development of Linwood.

Myra was well educated with the equivalent of a high school education. At 17 she moved from New York to East Saginaw with her parents in 1867, and at 21 married Mahlon and moved to Linwood to farm land that had been her family's lumber camp. She describes vividly the efforts to create the town of Linwood out of the cutover. We are told about clearing trees for the main street and building the first mill and general store. Despite the demands of being a farm wife, Myra still found time to have afternoon tea. The culture of the East was brought to the frontier by Myra. To keep the young men away from the pool halls, Myra organized a "Young People's Literary and Scientific Society," a town library, and a singing society. Although she died in 1892 at the age of 41, through her diaries, Myra Parsons left a legacy that a century later tells the real story of pioneer women.

FROM THE DIARY OF MYRA PARSONS:

Oct, 11, 1883: "J. McAllester died last night, from a peculiar accident, while logging he fell backwards, sitting down on a stub, tearing the organs in a shocking way, even breaking the water passage."

June 12, 1884: "Thurs. Harvey Danby lost his left hand at Linwood this A. M. about 9 A. M., was taken to Bay City on the 1:45 P. M. train, which they flagged at Linwood."

June 13, 1884: "We find Harvey Danby's hurt worse than we feared. The left hand cut off, flesh so torn the arm was taken off about the wrist joint, too bad, there was $103 raised for him at Linwood today."

January 16, 1885: "A serious accident happened on Town Line at the Swiss place. Some men were loading timber, when in some way Mr. McCuan's teamster was crushed. Dr. from Pinconning and two from Bay City [came] but the man was past help, dying about 9. P. M."

February 13, 1885: "Fri. Our french neighbor Billadou had the misfortune to split right hand open of a young frenchman who was helping him split cord wood."

June 6, 1885: "Fri. About 7 P. M. yesterday, P. L. Sherman had the misfortune to lose two fingers on left hand."

August 8, 1887: "Sat. Mr. Sherman's stave cutter Jack Wright lost a finger with stave knife."

November 19, 1887: "Sat. Sherman's mill not running today, men too drunk Mrs. Evans said.

August 8, 1890: "Tues. Will Evens came to tell us John Francis was hurt in woods, Log rolled over him breaking 5 ribs & injuring leg, he is at West Branch."

This is the German-American Sugar factory located at South Euclid and Kelton. Later, during World War I, it became the Columbia Sugar Co., and eventually the Monitor Sugar Company.

These workers are hand-harvesting corn on a company-owned, 150 acre, Bay County farm in 1927.

The milk wagon (above) arrives at a rural Bay County farm home, c. 1906. Many local creameries collected, processed, and delivered milk products to nearby rural communities.

A typical Bay County farmstead is shown below. "Fred and Henry in wagon, Joe, Jim, Frank, Kite, Ed, Martha, Larry and Paul" are identified in this otherwise unidentified photo.

Ittner's Corner

Ittner's Corner (or Willard) was a typical farming town with a general store, blacksmith's shop, a hotel, saloon, and some elevators. It was located at the corner of Eleven Mile and Beaver roads. This is the blacksmith's shop seen behind the hotel in the background in lower photo.

Ittner's Corner looking north down Eleven Mile Road. The general store (just recently torn down) is on the left, the Beaver Hotel (Willard Hilton) is facing the photographer, and the blacksmith's shop is in the distance.

Ittner's Corner General Merchandise store. The proprietor, G. R. Snyder (white shirt), and his wife, with camera taking photo of photographer, are in center, c. 1915.

Neighbors all came around to help raise the new barn in Munger in 1895. Note the young boys on beam in lumberjack fisticuffs pose.

A "birdseye" view of downtown Pinconning, 1915. Photo is taken from atop the chicory plant looking south down Kaiser and Manitou streets and the D & M Railroad tracks.

This is another, rural, agricultural settlement, Auburn, in western Bay County. M-20 or Midland Road is the main street in this 1939 photograph.

BAY CITY'S CHURCHES

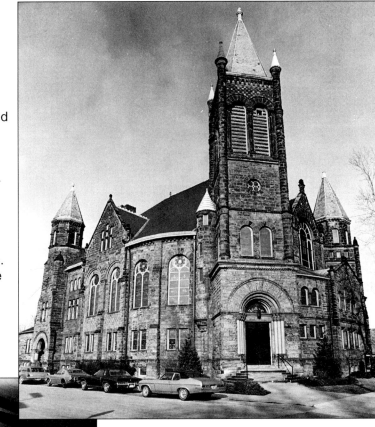

The First Presbyterian Church at Center and Jackson streets originated in 1848 and pioneer settlers James Birney and Judge Albert Miller were instrumental in establishing the congregation. Lumberman Alexander Folsom contributed the costs for the original, though smaller, structure. The church was also one of the first in the country to install women elders.

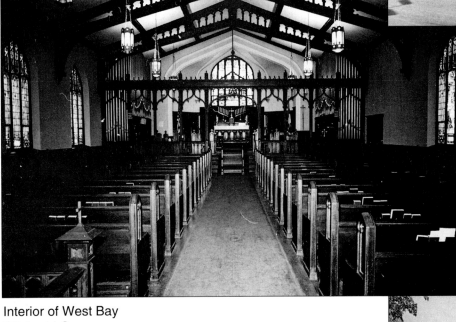

Interior of West Bay City's old Grace Episcopal Church. The Episcopal churches on the West Side were merged in 1965 to form St. Alban's Church.

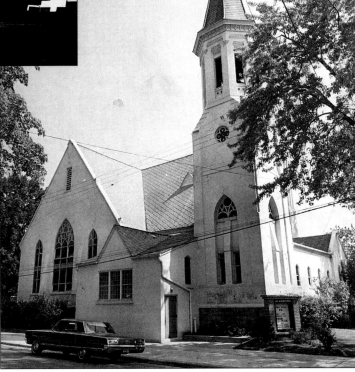

First Methodist Church at Wenona and Ohio. The Methodists were probably the first to organize church services in Bay County beginning with a Methodist meeting in 1837 and a circuit rider until 1845. Later on Methodist services were held inside of a lumber schooner pulled up along the river's edge.

Trinity Episcopal Church viewed from the outside, c. 1915. Trinity is one of the oldest congregations in Bay City dating back to 1842. William Fitzhugh one of Lower Saginaw's pioneer founders was an early lay leader of Trinity Church. Contributions came from several prominent early families in town to finance the construction of this building in 1887.

First Congregational Church at the corner of Sixth and VanBuren streets. The first congregation met in 1875 a few months prior to building the church seen here. The Congregationalists were spun-off in their initial organizational efforts from members of the First Presbyterian congregation.

First Baptist Church on the corner of Center and Madison was one of the oldest of Bay City's churches. Originally built in 1872, its two Gothic spires towered 130 and 180 feet. The bell was secretly installed one night to the surprise of the congregation as a gift from Mrs. James Fraser-McMaster shortly after the new church opened. The structure was removed in the 1970s, but the bell was relocated to the new church in Hampton Township.

St. Boniface Church and rectory were built primarily to serve the large German Catholic population settling in Bay City. It was located on Lincoln Avenue between 8th and 9th streets, and the original parish began in 1875-76.

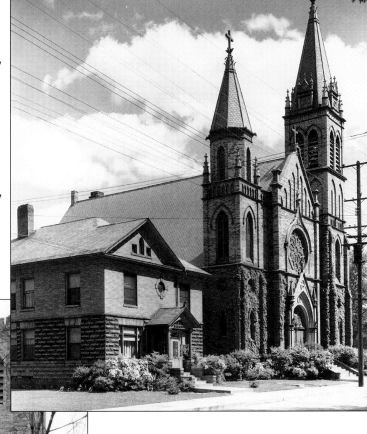

Zion Lutheran Church, in West Bay City at Ivy and Kiesel, was an offspring of the initial Lutheran congregation, St, Paul's in Frankenlust. Originally church members worshiped in a remodeled band hall on this site.

The original St. Stanislaus Catholic Church was a wooden structure erected in 1874, primarily through the efforts of Ludwig Danielewski, to serve the Polish community in south Bay City. Because the Poles worked as sawmill laborers, lumberman William Fitzhugh donated the land and Nathan Bradley pledged $500 dollars toward initial construction. This church at 22nd was replaced by the present building in 1892 located at 21st and Farragut.

EARLY SCHOOLS

No state in the Old Northwest carried on as well as Michigan did the directive in the Northwest Ordinance, "that schools and the means of education shall ever be encouraged."

While Bay City was still Lower Saginaw, in 1842, the first primary school district was organized and two schools opened in private homes—one in Portsmouth and the other in Lower Saginaw. In 1845, the first school house was built in Bay City at the corner of First and Washington.

Most early schools were single-room structures like the rural one-room, red school house. The school year was only about five months and children seldom went beyond the eighth grade. Early teachers were males, but by the 1860s females had replaced most men teachers. Though in the winter months, when more boys were in class, rural school districts preferred male teachers. Bay City's first high school opened on the East Side in 1869, on Grant between 9th and 10th Streets.

Wenona Graded School, June, 1873. Note the wooden sidewalks, and bell tower.

Recreational facilities were limited in early schools, but each tried to have teams for boys and girls. Here pictured is an early girls basketball team.

During the 1929-30 school year the city school system sponsored a city-wide spelling bee. This is the championship team from Washington School. In back: Norma Hawkins, Theresa MacMillan, Marian Buechler, Helen Davidson. In front, Walter VanLaam, Virginia Griffiths, Geraldine Gillis, Betty Smith, Meta Jane Criswell, and Fred Woolfitt.

Susie M. Crump's kindergarten class at the Riegel School in southeast Bay City, c. 1913. Kindergarten classes did not begin in Bay City until 1904. Miss Crump lived on Midland and Erie streets.

Mary S. Webster and her Fourth Grade class at the Corbin School, 1890. This was the first year that the school was in operation in West Bay City at Fulton and Walnut streets

Below is the Amelith School in Frankenlust Township in 1912. Mary A. Sharpe and A. C. Freeman are the teachers seated at each side of the class.

The First Bay City High School was located on Grant Street between 9th and 10th streets. After the new high school (below) was erected in 1882 the school was renamed Farragut School. This building was demolished in 1938.

When it closed in March of 1882, the students marched from the old high school to the new Eastern High on Madison near Columbus. It remained the high school for forty years until 1922 when Central High was opened. When this picture was taken several additions had already been made to the original building.

The Sims West Side Academy was located at William and John streets. An academy was often a private school for children attending beyond grade school.

This is the Dolsen School which was built in 1883, and was the first Bay City school in which kindergarten classes were held in 1904.

The Second Ward School after additions enlarged the school in the last quarter of the nineteenth century.

FUNERAL CUSTOMS

Life in the nineteenth century was often short and dangerous. Frequent deaths in the sawmills are one lumbering legacy that marked Bay City. Death was a common, everyday occurrence; something that was not unexpected. Men were killed in the forests, if not in sawmills, and children often died at birth or of illnesses that today are almost unknown. Women, because of the dangers of giving birth, frequently did not outlive their husbands as they do today.

Funeral customs were somewhat different at the turn of the century. The "Undertaker" performed the functions of today's funeral director, and before funeral parlors, the family's deceased were customarily laid out for one to three days in the home. A long black crepe was hung at the front door to let neighbors know that there had been a death in the family. Later the crepe was replaced by flowers or a dark wreath hung on the front door. At times, for prominent Bay Citians, a brass band led the funeral procession to the cemetery.

Prior to the use of the funeral home, the "undertaker" often embalmed the body in the home of the deceased where it was laid out for three days. The undertaker brought an elaborate box that was opened to provide mourning crepe and flowers that were traditionally laid around the casket. These customs began to disappear in the 1920s.

Death of a one-and-half-year-old Bay City child, 1899.

... FROM THE DIARY OF MYRA PARSONS

December 12, 1888:
I went to Mrs. Mank's at 9 A. M., took the baby soon after, and held it till it died at 11. A. M. dear little thing, how she suffered, think she had spinal trouble, I wrote note to Martin and Chamberlain for Casket, John Allman went for it, then I washed, dressed and laid out the baby, went to Linwood to see Elder Davis about holding services tomorrow.

December 13, 1888:
Began to snow at 9 A. M., soft, wet flakes that are far worse than rain. I went over and cleaned up house for Mrs. Mank dressed the baby, put her in casket. Mr. Glaspie took charge of the funeral, Prayer and music at house, sermon [sic] at schoolhouse, myself presiding at organ, After coming from grave I stopped there, straightened things around.

View of Pine Ridge Cemetery, 1888. It was established by pioneer James Birney around 1860 off Tuscola Road.

This is the first motor-driven hearse in Bay City owned by the W. S. Hyatt Funeral Home. c. 1913.

Entrance to Elm Lawn Cemetery. Elm Lawn was built on Ridge Road in 1890.

Fraternal Societies and Clubs

Fraternal societies and ethnic social clubs often offered members a "sense of belonging" to a group or community much like themselves and gave individuals comfort among like-minded fellow citizens. Masons, pioneer settlers, and women formed early clubs in Bay City. There was even an early Bachelor's Club that disbanded soon after half of its members married. Hunting and fishing clubs were popular among the well-to-do, and every ethnic group had its own local social organization. By 1900 there were a good number of secret societies like the Masons, Woodmen of the World, Elks, Knights of Pythias, Knights of Columbus, and others.

The Knights of Pythias gather for formal portrait in 1900. Note the Modern Woodmen of the World sign hanging above, left. This was also a fraternal organization of wood workers in and around Bay City.

The new Masonic Temple at Madison Avenue and Sixth was dedicated in 1893. The "handsomest temple in all the country," burned in 1903, but was quickly rebuilt.

The Masonic Temple in the Portsmouth area at 1619 Broadway.

Charter members of the Lady Macabees, organized November, 1890.

Bay City Kiwanis Club, father and daughter banquet, 1933.

Independent Order of Odd Fellows, a fraternal and benevolent secret society, met at the I. O. O. F. Hall at 314 Washington in 1939.

CHAPTER 6: BAY CITY LOGS ON

Executive bodies in Bay City allow no uncertain stone [business] to enter the foundation. All that is speculative or uncertain is discouraged, all that promised permanence is given substantial support.

Bay City Board of Trade, 1905

The high banks of the Kawkawlin River as they appeared in 1890. Water-laden logs rest along the banks as a memory to the log drives that ten years earlier fueled Bay City's lumber boom.

July 4, 1887! Despite the decline in lumber production, Bay City still manages to put on a grand Independence Day celebration. This is Center and Washington, looking west toward Water Street. The Phoenix block is on the left and under construction. Photo is from atop the Shearer building.

TRANSITION YEARS, 1890-1920

To the amazement of many people by 1888 all the pine in the Lower Peninsula had vanished. Bay City was faced with making an effort at the end of the white-pine era to sustain the community progress that had occurred so rapidly in the past two decades. Many absentee lumbermen in Bay City packed their men and equipment and moved west or to Canada. An attempt to keep the lumber business going was made by several local mill owners who rafted logs across Lake Huron from Canada. The Canadian government, though, stopped this practice in 1894 by declaring that logs cut in Canada must be processed there. Several Bay City firms then moved to Canada.

Between 1884 and 1900, Bay City lost less than ten percent of its population. Bay City's economic downturn was not as quick as Saginaw's or Muskegon's. The importation of Canadian logs, woodworking industries, shipbuilding, and fishing enabled Bay City to experience less trauma, although more than one half of its sawmills closed. However, gradual change in the economy of Bay City was unfortunate in one way because it did not compel the city's leadership to react to a life-or-death economic threat. Entrepreneurs diversified very conservatively into hardwood manufacturing and did not take risks in iron and steel-related industries. The Board of Trade, stung by the number of mills abandoned by absentee lumbermen, did not seek out-of-town investors or industries. Instead Bay City sustained itself well into the twentieth century by depending on wood-products manufacturing. This served its purpose during the transition period after lumbering, but with little heavy industry or diversified manufacturing, Bay City was not well-prepared for the modern industrial age.

On a warm July day in 1910, Midland Street on the West Side appears prosperous. Because of shipbuilding, coal, and sugar beets, West Bay City did not feel the end of the white-pine era as dramatically as Bay City. By 1910, shortly after unification of the two cities, the West Side likewise began to lose population.

NEW INDUSTRIES

Because of a loss of wood-related manufacturers, Bay City's work force declined in the immediate pre-World War I years. Most industries—like sugarbeets, fishing, shipbuilding, and wood-manufacturing—were often seasonal and offered only periodic employment.

Nevertheless some new firms did locate in Bay City between 1905 and 1920 and managed to sustain the economy. The North American Chemical Company purchased the old McGraw mill site and became one of the city's largest employers until it closed in 1927. William Clements' Industrial Works, the largest employer in the city after the turn of the century, prospered during the war years. Bay City Dredge Works, manufacturers of heavy equipment, shovels and cranes became the city's fourth largest employer in 1913. Shipbuilding enjoyed a partial revival when the Defoe Shipyard was opened in 1905.

An overview of the North American Chemical Company's plant in 1928, located at Harrison and 41st streets. North American used brine to manufacture chlorate and potash.

Industrial Works, later Brownhoist, manufactured cranes and heavy equipment. It was the city's largest employer in the post-lumber era. Here an IB crane for the New York, New Haven and Hartford Railroad lifts a test load of 150 tons.

This is a panoramic view of the Industrial Brownhoist plant along the river. By 1920 the Industrial Works had 1800 employees, occupied 29 acres and had 59 buildings.

However, woodworking manufacturers continued to employ most of the work force, while the automobile industry, represented by Union and Natco trucks, employed only a handful.

Two extractive industries that also provided employment during these transition years were the sugar beet and coal industries. Several sugar-beet processing factories were built early in the century to take advantage of the state bounty on production of sugar. The manufacturing of sugar required several thousand hands each fall, but it did not supply steady employment. Coal mining became important between 1900 and 1914. Yet, like sugar beets, employment was not steady and frequently went to experienced outsiders recruited from Ohio and Pennsylvania. By the late teens most of the mines, which could not compete with West Virginia coal in price or quality, shut down.

One of Bay City Dredge Works' first "land dredges" is shown above. This was built in 1914 and is seen operating in Hampton Township. It was used primarily for highway ditch construction and threw dirt only to one side. Note temporary rails being moved along by workers.

Shown below is a Trench Hoe manufactured by Bay City Shovels, 1926. In 1931 the Dredge Works became Bay City Shovels and was the city's fourth largest employer.

COAL MINING

Coal Mining once flourished in Bay County, especially early in the twentieth century. County coal was soft and somewhat expensive to mine because of the high water table, however, the demand for coal for home-heating, railroad steam locomotives, and prospective steel production encouraged large-scale mining in Bay and Saginaw counties.

In 1910, mines employed 1,600 men at 25 different sites in Bay County. New immigrant laborers and experienced hands from eastern coal mines moved into the area. Coal mining, though, remained a seasonal operation. Miners usually worked only 170 days a year, with peak production occurring in the winter months. Although boosting area employment, coal mining never provided the steady work of heavy manufacturing.

Diesel engines on locomotives, natural gas, home-heating oil, and the expense of digging out local soft coal all contributed to the gradual decline of production in Bay County. The peak coal-mining year was 1919; after that production went steadily downward. The last Bay County mine, the Begick mine, closed in 1947.

Workers in front of the Handy Mine as the main shaft was being built in 1900. The mine was the first in Bangor Township. Coal quality remained poor and the mines began to close in the 1920s.

The first mine in Bay County was the Michigan Mine in Monitor Township begun in 1897. A four-foot wide coal vein was struck and coal mining attracted a number of investors and migrant coal miners to the county.

Defoe Shipbuilding

In 1905, Harry J. Defoe, principal at Park school, quit his job and launched a new career in shipbuilding. Defoe began building small commercial fishing boats and knock-down boats that were sold and delivered throughout the world.

During World War I the U. S. Navy commissioned Defoe to build steel torpedo chasers and mine planters. The plant relocated to the East Side at the foot of Adams Street along the river. After the war, the company continued in operation building government rum-runner patrol craft and custom yachts. Perhaps the most famous boat built by Defoe was the presidential yacht used from the Eisenhower to Carter administrations.

During World War II Defoe grew rapidly; the U. S. Navy called upon the firm to build 156 vessels. Minesweepers, subchasers, destroyer escorts, landing craft, and Navy transport ships—one every seven days—were launched into the Saginaw River. Defoe employed 4,000 workers in the war years. In the post-war era the Bay City yard continued to manufacture destroyers, oceanographic research ships, 600-foot Great Lakes freighters, and for the Australian Navy, three destroyer escorts. The plant closed in late 1976 after Navy contracts disappeared, and the narrow river and its bridges prevented continued construction of the super carriers demanded by Great Lakes' shippers.

Harry J. Defoe

This is the *Barbara Ann*, a yacht built by Defoe in 1931 for S. L. Avery who was from Saginaw and Chairman of Montgomery Wards stores. Later it was used in World War II and in 1956 was assigned as the Presidential yacht. It was renamed the *Lenore, Honey Fitz,* and *Patricia* by Presidents Eisenhower, Kennedy, and Nixon.

An aerial view of the Defoe shipyards. Under construction, on the right, is the *Henry Wilson.* Defoe not only built Great Lakes steamships and yachts, but cargo carriers and hundreds of ships for the navy during the two World Wars.

During World War II, Defoe developed the revolutionary "roll-over" method of constructing ships. This enabled navy vessels to be built in the shipyard much more quickly with experienced welders working in an assembly line pattern where their work was close at hand. The hull was rolled over on the attached framework in three minutes.

BUSINESSES IN BAY CITY

Memories of the old family-run downtown stores and businesses were once again rekindled when the Knepps Department Store closed its doors recently. The wooden floors and glass display cases brought back nostalgic thoughts of all kinds of traditional mass merchandising methods employed a couple of generations ago in various Bay City businesses. The meat store had its "fresh" hanging produce on display and a sawdust-covered floor. The five-and-ten-cents stores, the

This is the jewelry store of Stephen Swart in West Bay City on the northwest corner of Linn and John streets. A one cylinder Cadillac is parked in front. Note that the time varies on the two clocks.

massive hardware emporiums, the old time barber shops, and the next-door cigar and drug stores are all part of the diverse business history of Bay City. Retailing is one facet of the local economy that has remained strong throughout the years. The out-town shopping malls have not as of yet devastated the neighborhood stores and downtown commercial center. There are more than two dozen enterprises that have remained in operation in Bay City for a century or more.

The Swan Johnson grocery and provisions store was on the corner of Thomas and Henry streets in West Bay City. Johnson was a Swedish immigrant who opened this store in 1882. He and his wife and three children lived above the store. The store still stands today.

Jennison Hardware is considered the oldest continuing business in Bay City dating back to 1850. This is the original building on Water Street that later burned down and was rebuilt. Note the tire sign on the roof.

The southwest corner of Center and Adams: Bay City Cash Dry Goods and the Woolworth's five-and-ten-cent store are to the right. The popular "cash store" was founded in 1882 by C. R. Hawley. This building was eventually demolished for the expanded Peoples' Bank.

Rosenbury & Sons was originally located at Fifth and Washington before moving to Third and Water streets. The Rosenbury furniture store was opened by C. E. Rosenbury in 1878. Taken in the late nineteenth century, this photo affirms the continuing prosperity of Bay City's retail industry in the post-lumber era.

Once the land was cut over in Bay County, much of it was put into agricultural use. Grist mills began to open in Bay City in the 1880s and 1890s. Here Bay City Flouring Mills on N. Water and First streets celebrate an export shipment of flour.

A. Lentz Boots and Shoes was at 510 Van Buren. Next door to the shoe store is the Lentz family residence.

The S. S. Kresge dimestore was a longtime fixture at the northeast corner of Center Avenue and Washington. This photo was taken in 1949.

This is a photograph of the 33 employees of the S. S. Kresge store taken just prior to the opening of the new store seen above in 1940.

The J. F. List Grocery store in Salzburg

Nuffer's General Merchandise store (below) was located on Salzburg Street in West Bay City.

Putz's Hardware store still stands on Salzburg near the river in West Bay City. Note the gas pumps in the 1920s photo.

Breen's Bicycle Shop and a cigar factory above the store were located at 304 N. Columbus.

Bay City, taking advantage of the available hardwoods, also became a center for manufacturing carriages and wagons. Here newly-built wagons leave the Toeppner Bro's. plant at 1905 Salzburg in West Bay City.

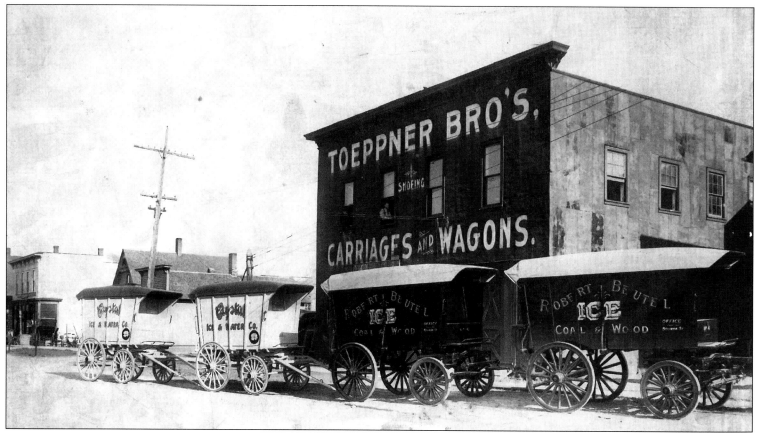

A. R. Maier Drug store at 1319 Third Street, 1890.

Store of C. H. Frantz, 407 Center Avenue. Henry Laidlaw, "soda jerk" leans against the post, Albert Meire is in back of mailbox, and C. H. Frantz is in the center.

Tupper Drugstore at 211 N. Walnut. Frank Tupper, Harriet Tupper, Dr. K. Dishon, Mrs. Ed MacIntosh, Dr. Waller, Frank MacIntosh, Roy MacIntosh (boy) and Mr. Brown (in front) are pictured.

SUGAR BEET MANUFACTURING

The decline of lumbering prompted several Bay City business and newspapermen to encourage the growth and manufacturing of beet sugar in the mid 1890s. Bay City investors quickly built three processing plants and encouraged area farmers to plant beets from fence row to fence row. However, by 1904, too many factories and too many sugar-beet farms forced several processing plants to close. Later, only after smaller operators merged into the Michigan Sugar Company in Carrollton and Monitor Sugar on Bay City's West Side, did beet-sugar manufacturing return a profit. The Monitor Sugar Company was founded in 1932 as a subsidiary corporation of the Robert Gage Coal Co. Originally this West-Side plant was the German-American Sugar Company, and later (1917) the Columbia Sugar Company. In the 1930s, over 60,000 farmers grew sugar beets in Michigan. Today the state produces about one-half million pounds of sugar annually and involves about 2,400 farmers.

The Mendal J. Bialy Sugar Company in West Bay City was located at Roy and Prairie streets and was one of the pioneer beet-sugar processors, beginning in 1900.

Sugar beet workers were hired in the fall months and generally worked through the beginning of the following year. Because of overproduction, many plants were forced to close as early as 1905.

WHAT IS A SUGAR BEET?

Although it is a rare sugar beet that grows to the size of that Bay County beet pictured below, the soil in the valley is capable of providing beets with a high sugar content. The fleshy root of the sugar beet is second only to sugar cane among important sources of sugar. The plant has a large cluster of bright green leaves, or crown, and the beet is the enlarged upper part of its root. It weighs two or more pounds and has a tap root that can grow seven feet into the soil. The sugar beet is actually a biennial because it takes two years for the plant to develop flowers and branches. Of course it is usually dug up after the first year and sent to the refinery.

Sugar is taken from the beets by washing the beets and cutting them into thin slices with revolving knives. The slices are placed in vats of hot water that soak the sugar from the beets. The beet sirup is purified, filtered, and boiled into sugar crystals which are then dried, granulated and packaged. Newcomers to the valley should never drive too close behind a sugar-beet truck in the fall months, and should never run over a three-pound sugar beet lying in the road.

"Knocked-down Housing"

After the white pine was cut in Michigan, more than eight million acres of hardwood remained along the Saginaw River's tributaries. Much of this was put to use in the sawmills building flooring and smaller boats. In 1906, William J. Sovereign and his brother Otto E., came up with the idea of using the knock-down method, applied to barrel shooks and small boats, to build small, redi-cut cottages and garages for shipment as a kit for on-site assembly. They began to market the homes under the name "Aladdin Homes" named after the "Aladdin" in the Arabian Nights story whose genie built a castle overnight. Redi-cut homes supposedly could be put up in one day. Aladdin later built larger homes and lasted as a separate company in Bay City until 1982.

The Lewis Manufacturing Company cut wood for the Aladdin firm in its early years, but when Aladdin opened its own sawmill Lewis opened its own mail-order home business. "Lewis Built Homes," later renamed "Liberty Homes," manufactured houses in Bay City from 1914 to 1973. A third redi-cut home manufacturer in Bay City was International Mill and Timber which built "Sterling Homes" from 1916 to 1971.

For awhile in the middle of the twentieth century, Bay City had three redi-cut home manufacturers which made it the nation's center for precut homes. A nation-wide advertising effort, especially by Aladdin Homes, coupled with reasonable prices (as seen here in the 1930s listings catalogue), and quality construction brought considerable success. Aladdin, located on Water and Belinda, Lewis Manufacturing and International Mill and Timber made Bay City, by 1950, the national center for prefabricated housing. All three firms eventually discontinued operation between 1971 and 1982.

The Finley — $841.70
Price, $886
Cash discount, 5%
Net price, $841.70

WHILE the Finley is popular with the owner of any sized lot, yet it finds special favor in cities where lots are sometimes as narrow as 30, or even 25 feet. The Finley can be built very nicely on a 25-foot lot and still leave ample space for a walk on either side.

In the Finley the architect has followed throughout plain, straight lines, yet when painted French gray or leather brown and trimmed in white, the owner of the Finley is invariably delighted.

A large, pleasant front porch, six rooms, bath and closettes are found in this remarkably low priced house. The ever popular plan is followed of a large living room across the entire front with wide archway leading to dining room. By a double-action door one enters the kitchen direct from the dining room. An attractive semi-open stairs leads from living room to second floor where there are to be found three sleeping rooms, bath and closettes. Those wanting a six-room, two-story plain house are invariably pleased with the Finley.

On an average, owners of the Finley claim savings of $200 to $325 on their homes. These estimates include savings on cost of material, also savings on cost of labor. When you receive the material it is entirely cut-to-fit, ready for erection. You pay for only the actual material used in building your home—no more. Now, think of the good lumber that is wasted in building the old-fashioned way. And you also pay for the extra labor which is unnecessary building an Aladdin.

LATER INDUSTRIAL DEVELOPMENT: AUTOMOBILES AND CHEMICALS

The automobile industry, during the 1920s and 1930s, spurred the development of auto-parts manufacturing in Bay City. Efforts at manufacturing several trucks were made in the post-war years. In 1911 the National Cycle Company began to build automobile parts and later attempted to put together a truck called the "Natco" (National Motor Truck Company). While the manufacture of Natco Trucks did not succeed, the parts plant flourished. In 1916 it was bought by Chevrolet Motor Company and has continued to make parts for automobiles right up until the present time as G. M. Powertrain Division.

In 1912 there was a brief effort to manufacture an automobile in Bay City called the "Winonah," but this concern apparently never produced a car for the market. The Union Truck Company, organized in 1916, began to produce trucks and later buses at a new plant on Patterson near the river. The company built trucks until 1927 when, after a series of financial pitfalls, it dissolved. The other important industry that spun off from auto-manufacturing was the Electric Auto-Lite Company. The Bay Division was started in 1936 at the foot of Morton Street in Salzburg. It was opened through the efforts of the Chamber of Commerce which pledged $75,000 to bring the plant to Bay City from Toledo. As Prestolite it became the second largest employer in Bay City, and manufactured various electrical parts for automobiles until it closed in the 1980s.

Dow Chemical Company purchased the Union Truck manufacturing plant on Patterson and in 1934 began to build light haulaway trailers out of magnesium manufactured by Dow. Dow later added two additional manufacturing plants in Bay City. Several electric companies also later located in Bay City—Kuhlman Electric and Resistance Welding—to build transformers and electric welding machines. By mid-century, Bay City had reestablished a substantial economy base and its population passed its lumber-era peak—reaching 57,504 in 1950.

Workers gather outside of the National Cycle Company's buildings. In 1892 the company was started by Henry B. Smith and eventually was shipping thousands of "National" bicycles throughout the country.

A catalog page depicting one of 8-10 bike models sold by National Cycle in the World War I era.

NATIONAL CHAINLESS CUSHION FRAME MODEL 69
Price $80.00 Cash

SPECIFICATIONS

FRAME—22 inches high, made from 1-inch seamless tubing, with patented cushion in rear stays.
FRONT FORKS—Crown, drop forged of our own design, taper gauge fork sides, specially made for us.
ENAMEL—National Blue, plain.
WHEELS—28-inch diameter, with teak-finished rims striped with blue.
TIRES—National single tube, 1½-inch diameter.
CRANKS—6½ inches long, tempered.
GEAR—72 inches. PEDALS—Rubber. SADDLE—No. 5.
HANDLE BAR—No. 4 with round leather grips.

OPTIONS

FRAME—24 inches high.
ENAMEL—National Red or Black; plain or decorated.
GEAR—82 inches.
TIRES—Goodrich, G. & J. or Palmer.
EXTRAS—Cinch Coaster and Brake in rear hub $5.00.
National Spring Fork $5.00.

The National Cycle Company's office and plant was a red, two-story structure located near Woodside between Crotty and Madison. By 1896, 5,000 "wheels" were made, and in 1909 National began to build car parts for Packard and Studebaker automobiles.

In 1913, National began to build "Natco" trucks in a newly-built manufacturing plant on the site of the old bicycle building. Fewer than 25 trucks were manufactured when Smith decided to abandon trucks and stick with bicycles and auto parts. In 1916 William Durant bought the National plant and began to build parts for his Chevrolet automobile.

This is on the site of the old National Cycle Company's plant when Chevrolet is undertaking an early expansion program. In 1928 the remaining National buildings were torn down and a new two million dollar Chevy plant erected. The Powertrain Division remains the largest employer in the city and produces some 200 separate auto parts.

The first automobile came to Bay City in 1895. It was reportedly brought to town by Hi Henry on a promotional tour for his minstrel show. The "horseless carriage" was kept under lock and key and guarded in a barn at 5th and Saginaw streets.

In 1916 the Union Truck Company was organized in Bay City and located along Patterson Street near the river. It continued to build various models of trucks (like the one above) and buses until it failed in 1927.

Oswald Auto Company was located on North Walnut in West Bay City. Peter J. Oswald sold and repaired automobiles and also small gasoline engines. The 1915 Studebaker, seen here, was a 50 horsepower model with six cylinders and cost $1,000.

In 1937 Dow Chemical's magnesium foundry moved to Bay City, and its work force grew until during World War II, 3,300 were employed. The company purchased the old Union Truck Company buildings on Patterson. During the war years Dow manufactured magnesium castings and assemblies for aircraft.

A U. S. Army "Mutt" containing several Prestolite parts viewed in 1967. The Auto-Lite plant was brought here from Toledo by civic leaders in 1936 during the Great Depression. By 1938 Auto-Lite employed nearly 1,300 people at its Morton Avenue plant on the West Side. The "Mutt" contained Prestolite parts including the headlights, underwater starting motor, and bulk wiring. The plant closed in the 1980s.

This is Washington Avenue looking north along the east side of the street between 4th and 5th streets. In the distance at left is the new post office (1893) and Harman and Verner, well-known photographers in Bay City.

Political Readjustments

Economic decisions—especially those involving the reindustrialization of Bay City in the post-lumber era—were not made in a political vacuum. When lumbermen took their financial interests elsewhere, they abdicated their political, as well as their economic, responsibility to lead Bay City beyond the white-pine era. As a result of this lack of leadership, in a city already known for labor rancor and its concentrated immigrant populations, a great deal of turmoil and turnover developed in city politics.

The main stone carving over the entrance of City Hall represents city industries: a brine well, an anchor, a band and circular saw blades, and a catch of fish.

Even though they had organized during the 1885 Ten-Hour Strike, workers in Bay City never successfully transferred this new-found power into organized politics during the last fifteen years of the century. Labor unions as well as immigrants went back and forth voting between "Republican-Labor" and "Democrat-Labor" tickets. Lumbermen in Bay City failed to take advantage of this in-fighting and division among the labor bloc. They stayed away from politics, and between 1885 and 1910, only two of ten mayors were lumbermen. One of these, George H. Shearer, owned a small mill and sympathized with the strikers in 1885. Because the city's economic leaders seldom involved themselves in local politics, doctors, lawyers, small businessmen, and professional politicians controlled the city's elective offices. These individuals were not motivated to protect the city's large-scale economic interests. Political scientists characterized Bay City's government in those years, as providing mere "caretaker" functions. Little city-building was evident during the transition years.

Bay City's lumbering families not only abdicated responsibility when it came to the city's economic and political future, they also resisted public efforts that were made, though infrequently, to modernize the city.

An analysis of voting patterns at the ward level between 1883 and 1903 suggests that the wealthy areas of the community consistently voted against proposed bond issues for urban improvements. On four bond issues—citywide public lighting, a new city hall, a new farmers' market, and a referendum on uniting Bay City and West Bay City—the two wards off Center Avenue consistently voted no. In contrast, the working-class and ethnic wards supported all bonding issues with large majorities. Apparently people of wealth in Bay City were not only reluctant to reinvest in the declining milltown, they also remained unwilling to be taxed to pay for public improvements.

The interaction of politics, business, and labor was also evident in the struggle to consolidate the two communities on either side of the river. With the decline of lumbering, taxes for schools, sidewalks, sewers, and the duplication of city services were considered expensive. It seemed only natural, especially to businessmen, that the cities combine to save resources. Between 1889 and 1890 efforts were made to unite West Bay City and Bay City. West Bay City, which was economically dominated by Sage and the shipyards of Wheeler and Davidson, continued to prosper in the immediate post-lumber period. Local leaders convinced many West Siders that annexation would lead to higher taxes as civic improvements were legislated by the more populated East Side. Three votes for consolidation were defeated on both sides of the river by voters in 1887, 1890, and 1897.

Not until 1903 did the two towns vote to unite, and even then opponents to consolidation introduced a "repeal" bill in the state legislature. The bill passed both state houses; however, a committee of businessmen from both towns persuaded the governor to veto the repeal bill. Finally, greater Bay City was created in 1905, but it took two more years of haggling to work out a compromise city charter.

In the next 25 years Bay City's government went through a number of structural changes. In 1920 the city adopted a city-manager form of government and elected five commissioners at large instead of the previous two from each of nine wards. At-large elections did not set well with many strong neighborhood and immigrant groups, and in 1929, ward representation was reestablished. In 1933, again nine wards were drawn each with one commissioner. Because of ethnic neighborhoods, strikes and labor troubles, cross-river rivalries, and little citywide leadership, several of Bay City's wards developed strong personal leaders. Individualistic neighborhood representatives did not envision the benefits of city-building. Bay City became, as the *Bay City Tribune* pointed out in the early twentieth century, "a city of huddled homes separated into several communities."

Far left: In order to keep county farms in operation most cities in the late nineteenth century built farmers' markets to enable local farmers to bring produce directly to market. Bay City's was built through a bond issue in the 1890s, and was located between Washington and Saginaw, south of Second.

Left: From 1857 to 1869 county supervisors met in a rented building at the river and Fourth Street. In 1869 they moved to a new building at the site of the present Bay County Building. The building pictured here was constructed in 1933 at the corner of Madison and Center. It was a jobs project during the Great Depression and was funded by a city approved bond of $375,000. The building was opened in March, 1934, and today stands out for its art deco modern architecture. The building was designed by Joseph G. Goddeyne and for that era was considered, at eight stories, a skyscraper.

City Hall

As the post-lumber era began, cities in the 1890s often engaged in campaigns to rebuild downtown areas into more attractive places in order to bring in new industries and residents. The "City Beautiful" movement affected Bay City, and, in 1889 after considerable haggling over a site, citizens approved a $40,000 bond for a new City Hall.

Pratt & Koeppe, a local architectural firm, designed the exterior in Romanesque Revival, a popular style of the era. Additional costs delayed completion of the building until 1897. For years the new City Hall was a proud and recognizable landmark in Bay City. However, like other late-nineteenth century buildings,—the Washington Street Post Office and Michigan Central Depot—the City Hall began to feel its age. The sandstone exterior turned black from coal-fired boilers, and the interiors became obsolete. Most of these once-beautiful buildings in Bay City were demolished.

Although replacement with a new, modern building was seriously considered, several far-sighted leaders convinced city government to rehabilitate the old structure. At a total cost of $3.1 million, between 1976 and 1982 the entire building, inside and out, was restored. The tower clock, which had not operated in decades, was replaced, and new roof tiles were laid on the tower. The restoration effort and the "new" City Hall are accomplishments that Bay City can indeed look upon with pride. City Hall is a landmark everyone continues to recognize and reflects Bay City's past grandeur.

The entrance to City Hall prior to renovation between 1976 and 1982.

Bay City's City Hall at Washington and Tenth in the early twentieth century.

Legend Check: CITY HALL LEGENDS

Several interesting stories and legends are associated with Bay City's City Hall. Reportedly it is located on what was once an Ojibwa meeting site where tribal business was conducted. The site was also originally considered, in the 1890s, too far from town and amid too many fine homes and churches for a rancorous city government to conduct business.

During the building of the new structure, in 1894, a young boy, Robbie Waldo, slipped and fell to his death while placing roofing tiles. Robbie was just short of his 12th birthday, and his death encouraged the city to enact early laws to prevent children under the age of 16 from working in heavy industry and construction.

The tower clock, which was water operated, made Ripley's "Believe it or Not" years ago. It was claimed that fish from the river were sucked into the clock's gears and made it inoperative. For decades the clock's hands stood at two past nine o'clock. In 1976, an electronic clock replaced the inoperative clock and the brass bells, which had been taken down in 1952, were replaced by an electric carillon system.

The Armory and The "Bull Moose"

The structure that currently houses the Bay County Museum is the second armory building to occupy the site. The old, block-long wooden building that originally stood there was better known as the "home" for Spanish-American War veterans. It was also remembered for its dance hall, roller skating, parties, bowling lanes, boxing matches, and inside circuses. In the winter the floor was flooded and allowed to freeze for "indoor" ice skating.

The present armory building was erected around 1910. It is famous as a national landmark because the first split in the Republican Party between supporters of Theodore Roosevelt and President William Howard Taft occurred here in April of 1912.

The G. O. P.'s state-wide convention met in Bay City in April of that year, and the armory was the convention's headquarters. Quickly Taft and Roosevelt men in the delegation divided into two warring factions. The entire affair became so raucous that fist fights broke out. Locked out of the armory, Roosevelt's backers fought their way in through the windows. When the Bay City police failed to keep order, the Governor ordered the state militia into the city to bring order to the Grand Old Party. Eventually, the Roosevelt faction met separately in the armory and nominated its own delegation. At the national Republican Convention later that summer in Chicago, Roosevelt's delegates were refused recognition. They bolted the meeting and organized the Progressive, or "Bull Moose," Party and nominated T. R. for President against Taft. Hence, the first faction of the Progressive Party was organized in Bay City's National Guard Armory.

The original Armory was a block-long wooden building located at Washington and Ninth streets next to City Hall.

The new National Guard Armory building was built sometime around 1910, and presently houses the Bay County Museum.

This photo was taken during the 1912 Republican State Convention that was held in Bay City at the Armory. During the meeting the supporters of Theodore Roosevelt were prevented from entering the hall and only gained admission by climbing through the first-floor windows. The squabble became so intense that the Republican Governor was forced to call up the state militia to bring order to the delegates.

Post Office

The area's first post office was established in Portsmouth in 1837 with Judge Albert Miller as postmaster. Wenona had a post office in 1865, and Lower Saginaw in 1846. In the Civil War era the Bay City post office was located at Third and Water but later moved to the Westover Building on the southwest corner of Center and Washington.

In 1893, as part of the "City Beautiful" movement, an elaborate Romanesque post office was built—at the cost of $200,000—by the U. S. Government on a cleared site where the present-day federal building stands. This was one of the most attractive new buildings in town rivaling in style and grandeur the soon-to-be-completed City Hall. In 1931 this building was replaced by the current federal building.

From 1886 until 1893 the Bay City post office was located on Washington Avenue in the McEwan Block until it moved to a new federal building erected on the site of the present post office.

This is the interior of the Romanesque style U. S. Post Office building in Bay City in 1915. Henry Lutzke is seated in foreground.

Mail carriers stand in front of the old West Bay City post office. About this time, 1882, Bay City began to number houses in order to facilitate free mail delivery.

Bay City postal carriers gather proudly in front of the old downtown post office in 1915.

After moving around to several locations the federal government finally built a rather grand Romanesque style post office and Federal Building on Washington between 3rd and 4th streets in 1893. This building was in turn torn down and replaced by the present Federal Building in 1931.

Rural Free delivery was begun in 1896, and while it brought about the end to many small postal stations in rural towns, delivery to farmers was soon taking place daily. Here Fred Anderson delivers the mail in 1918 along his Midland Road route.

BRIDGES? THOSE "%@$*&" BRIDGES!

Mothers often remind children at those oh-so-boring family get-togethers that "if you cannot talk about anything, talk about the weather." In Bay City, mothers encourage their offspring to "talk about the city's bridges." There is probably no other discussion topic in Bay City that inevitably brings universal agreement, and consternation, than past and present bridges. Heat, electrical problems, and ship collisions seem to keep one or more of the city's bridges in need of constant repair. Bay City drivers finger their rosaries patiently at every bridge opening (or closing).

A history of the legal entanglements, locations, and closings of Bay City's bridges would necessitate a short book. The original first bridge—the Third Street structure—would itself fill several chapters. This bridge replaced a rope ferry that connected the two downtowns in 1865. It was rebuilt several times—its parts often salvaged to build other bridges upriver—and finally collapsed in 1976. Until the four-lane Veterans bridge was opened in 1957, motorists had only the links at Lafayette Street and Third Street to get downtown. The Independence and Liberty bridges now provide much better access and connections that have brought East and West Sides together.

The old Belinda Street Bridge opened in 1893. After rusted rivets began to pop out, a new four-lane structure, the Independence Bridge, replaced the old bridge, pictured here, in 1977.

The old wooden bridge crossing the Kawkawlin River, c. 1890.

The freighter, *Robert C. Norton,* passes through the Lafayette Street Bridge.

The first bridge across the Saginaw River was at Third Street built in 1865. A steel bridge replaced the old wooden Third Street Bridge in 1876. It was rebuilt in 1889, in 1919, again in 1925, and in 1958. The bridge approaches on both sides of the river were the most active places in Bay City and prime real estate property.

The Third Street Bridge was a toll bridge until 1883. It cost three cents to walk across or for a one-horse wagon. Two-horse teams were assessed six cents. In 1867, total tolls were $10,000. Pictured here is the bridge tender.

On June 18, 1976, the old two-lane Third Street Bridge gave up the ghost and collapsed after swinging open for a freighter. It took months to remove the wreckage and ten years to decide on the location and size of the replacement structure at Vermont Street and Woodside.

Disasters!

Living at the mouth of a river with nearly 900 miles of tributaries, and in a climate where "100-year rains" come somewhat more frequently, doubtlessly leads to periodic flooding in Bay City. Bay City has been fortunate to escape most damaging consequences of high waters that have plagued the Saginaw River Basin. The 1904 and 1986 floods were probably the worst, engulfing much of the Southend, Portsmouth, and Frankenlust. Other disasters associated with the river and bay include bridges collapsing, fires, ice jams removing houses, and an interurban train wreck on the bridge south of town near Cheboyganing Creek. Thirteen people were killed when the intercity train plunged off the bridge left open after a ship's passing.

On July 7, 1897 the Interurban between Bay City and Saginaw ran through the Saginaw River bridge that was inadvertently left open. The disaster took place on the river just south of Cheboyganing Creek. Thirteen people were killed and many seriously injured. Divers were lowered in the murky depths to recover the dead.

Perhaps the worst flood prior to 1986 to occur in Bay City struck in 1904. An extremely cold winter, heavy snows, frozen rivers and sudden rains plunged much of south Bay City underwater. This is at 37th and Ingraham streets looking west.

Flooding began on March 25, 1904 and lasted almost eight days. Ice jams at bridges forced the river over its banks. Several people died during the rampage upriver in Saginaw. In this photo the residence of William Lord, Harrison and 38th streets, is inundated.

An all-too-familiar sight, a Michigan snowstorm hits Bay City. This is at Third and Water streets, looking across the old Third Street Bridge.

Northeasterly winds and thick ice are an unfortunate combination for many who live along the bay's eastern shore. Forest Wiles examines ice damage to his bayside residence in 1961.

On July 5, 1915, disaster struck the Bay City fire department when its recently purchased truck, pictured above, was hit by a Michigan Central Railroad train crossing Wenona Avenue on the West Side. Two firemen were killed and several others seriously injured.

Early Sports

Bay City can look back with pride on its sports history and its athletes' accomplishments. Baseball was probably the first organized sport in the lumber era. Teams representing breweries, shipyards, and other industries competed on make-shift playing fields. The first professional baseball team was organized in Bay City in 1882, and played in various leagues until the World War I years.

Football became popular when an intense rivalry began between Bay City's old Eastern and Western high schools in the early twentieth century. Basketball was primarily a school activity in its early years until it expanded with city recreational teams in the 1930s. Boxing at the Armory flourished at the beginning of the century. Later, bouts were also held at the Clements Airport hangar. Bay City has also been proud of its success at launching several statewide tennis champions.

Above: Eastern High School's girls basketball team, 1910.

Above right: Farmer's Hunting group at Oak Grove, Aug. 4, 1898.

Right: Lumbermen and others who could afford the investment, loved the challenge of a good horse race. Bay City's barons often saw horse racing as an exclusive sport, and they tried often to attract the Grand Circuit to the old fair grounds where only the best horses competed and crowds of several thousand were common.

Bay City was always known as a great baseball city and many of the local teams were sponsored by community businesses. Barnstorming teams of independents frequently came to town and challenged the local nine. Games were staged on Sunday afternoons at the old Clarkston Park on Center near Livingston at the fairgrounds area. Pictured is Chatfield Milling Grain Company's team.

Professional and semi-pro baseball teams flourished until the years of the Great Depression when sponsorships dried up and one by one the teams disappeared.

The West Bay City "Wanderers Football" Team (or soccer team?), pose for this rather intriguing photo with S. O. Fisher's home in background in 1897.

CHAPTER 7: WARS, DEPRESSION AND PROSPERITY

> *"Bay County can be proud of the way it has responded whenever our democracy was threatened. Its men—and women, too—have never been shy or backward offering their services to this country."*
> **The Land and Its People**

BEYOND LUMBERING

Shortly before the beginning of World War I, the U. S. Census Bureau conducted a review of manufacturing in Bay City. The report noted: "The lumber industry still predominates, and that manufacturing increased only 14.2 percent during the previous decade." While other former lumbertowns, which had created more diversified manufacturing jobs, grew rapidly during the war years, Bay City's dependence on wood-related industries kept war-time growth at a more moderate pace. Between 1910 and 1920, Bay City added 2,388 people, and although its manufacturing tripled, the town still did not regain lumber-era momentum.

Nonetheless, with the arrival of several successful new industries like North American Chemical, Defoe's shipyards, and Bay City Dredge Works, prosperity was sustained and Bay City remained a pleasant community of churches, families, and neighborhoods. The loss of wood-related industries in the post-war years brought the economy to a low ebb in early 1920, but in the next decade—the "Roaring Twenties"—unprecedented expansion in automobile-parts production, pre-cut housing, shipbuilding, and cranes and shovels soon spurred the city's economy to new heights.

While the Great Depression did not hit Bay City immediately, by 1932 nearly 50 plants had closed and the reality of unemployment, mortgage foreclosures, banks shutting down, and bread lines became a part of almost everyone's life in town. Although the worst was over by 1934, for the entire decade, one could periodically see homeless, ragged men on the streets of Bay City or neighbors standing on the corner in the morning waiting for the WPA truck.

In 1941, with the on-coming World War, prosperity returned to Bay City. By 1950 the town's population reached 57,504. The end of the war brought hope and expectations; prosperity spurred growth out of the city and into suburban townships. Bay Citians could look back on the first half of the twentieth century with contentment. They had weathered the storms of wars and depression, and finally established a durable economy that was to guarantee the next generation prosperity and comfort. Bay City had at last evolved beyond the lumber legacy.

Bay City continued to rebuild in the post-lumber era. One of the steps taken to make the city more attractive to new residents was to remove abandoned lumber yards and unsightly buildings from the waterfront. Part of that plan included a new waterfront park, Wenonah Park, being laid out here in 1911.

The Spanish-American War, 1898

Normally the Spanish-American War goes unreported in the annals of community history. However, in Bay City, largely because of the war record and writings of Augustus Gansser, there is much to remember about the contributions of Bay City men during the struggle to free Cuba from Spain in 1898.

Gansser, who was a sergeant in the local militia unit—the Peninsulars Military Company, later Company C, 33rd Michigan Volunteer Regiment—wrote a history of local regimental activities in Cuba. He also penned a history of Bay County in 1908. Today the 33rd Regiment's tattered American flag still hangs in the Bay County Building.

About 100 Bay City men volunteered to fight in Company C in 1898. Two local sailors were killed in the blast that destroyed the battleship *Maine* prior to the outbreak of hostilities in April. By July, the 33rd was in Cuba (after training at Camp Eaton near Brighton) and in the thick of battle to take the city of Santiago. Later, after the battle, the 33rd was assigned to guard Spanish prisoners. The climate was "the most miserable on earth," wrote Bay City Private Emil Hartig. Everyone wanted to return home. Many of the men came home sick with malaria and fever; 19 local soldiers died in the campaign. On September 3, 1898, the city put on a grand reception for the Peninsulars when they arrived back in town after their recovery and victory in Cuba.

Spanish-American War soldier, Albert E. Meisel (center), is pictured here in 1898. Meisel was a railroad millman for decades and died in Bay City in 1952.

Michigan's Spanish-American War, Company C, 33rd Regiment from Bay City, relaxes during training operations, 1898.

Bay City's 33rd Regiment established the Michigan National Guard's first Hospital Corps during the War, seen here in 1898.

World War I and the Homefront

Even before the United States entered World War I in April of 1917, Bay City's 33rd Regiment was sent to Mexico with General Pershing in an unsuccessful attempt to capture Pancho Villa. Maj. Gansser was in command of the 33rd in 1917 when it was ordered to Battle Creek to construct a training facility named Camp Custer. Gansser was director of operations there until late summer of 1917.

In October, the 33rd Regiment was sent to Texas and joined with Wisconsin guardsmen to form a new 32nd or "Red Arrow" Division. A second Bay City company, the 128th Ambulance, was also part of the Red Arrow brigade. Bay City's two companies were sent to France in January of 1918, and fought in most of the major campaigns against the Germans.

The Red Arrow Division was credited with major roles in four separate offensives against 23 German army divisions. They took a total of over 2,000 prisoners, and were among the first U. S. troops to move into Germany in 1918. Sixteen men from Bay City in the Red Arrow Division won Medals of Valor.

At home, war fever spilled over into blatant big-

Pictured in front of Bay City's original Armory Building, located at the site of second armory building (Bay County Museum), is Company C of the 33rd Infantry, Michigan National Guard, c. 1895. In World War I the 33rd joined with Wisconsin guardsmen to form the famous 32nd or Red Arrow Division.

otry against many in the large German population that lived in Bay County. Germans remained proud of their homeland and despite the war some Lutheran churches and homes flew the German flag. Patriotism fanned the coals of hate and it was not uncommon for Germans to lose their jobs or incur injury. Mail to Germany was suspended, and everything German, including language instruction in public schools, was forbidden. The German-American Sugar Company and other businesses quietly changed their names.

While the end of the War on November 11, 1918, brought peace, it brought little celebration to Bay City. On November 9, there were five deaths from the flu epidemic in Bay City. Over 1,370 local cases closed schools and all other public places. Many of those who celebrated on November 11, did so while wearing surgical masks and wracked with fever. Lines of horsedrawn hearses stood along Jackson Street awaiting bodies from Samaritan Hospital. Forty-two people died in November alone, and the epidemic only began to subside in the following year after a total of 322 deaths.

Maj. Augustus H. Gansser was in command of the 33rd in 1917.

Four Bay Citians pose for a studio photograph prior to embarking for France in 1917. Included in photo is Victor Constineau.

Charles King, on left, poses with a friend in this World War I photo. Studio photographs were common remembrances sent to families prior to service overseas in 1917.

Bay City military parade in 1918 after World War I.

In 1926, the ship, *Witch,* lays flowers along the Saginaw River in memory of the soldiers lost in World War I.

Women were recruited into the work force in Bay City during World War I because of the scarcity of male employees. Here at the Wilson Body Company, on Farragut Street, women are making fabric covering for airplane bomber parts in 1917.

THE ROARING TWENTIES

The return to normalcy after World War I sometimes seemed to mean that the idealism of the war years was lost in the quest to get rich. Prosperity returned to Bay City in the 1920s as new industries located in the city and automobile parts production greatly expanded. Car production accelerated from one million a year in 1919 to over four and one-half million by 1929. There were soon 23 million cars on the road, and this stimulated entire new industries—road building, suburban development, car services, motels, cottages and other recreational businesses. Because of its location and experience in building redimade cottages, fishing, and boat-building, Bay City did well in the Roaring Twenties. Although farmers, coal miners, and textile workers in Bay City did not often participate in the new-found prosperity, industrial workers did well even if part of their success was based on credit and a working wife. As additional workers came into Bay City new subdivisions began to expand outside the city.

Prohibition also characterized the 20s, and with it came a loss of respect for law and order as bootleggers and crime bosses became prosperous and powerful. Women had recently gained the right to vote and with the new-found freedom of the twenties, they bobbed their hair, shortened their skirts, and began to smoke cigarettes. Traditional moral values seemed to be in decline. All of this led to fear and repression. New immigrants were not welcomed and minorities found it difficult to work in local industries. Bay City toyed with the Ku Klux Klan as the movement spread throughout the state espousing traditional, white American values. All of this—the roaring twenties and the imagined collapse in values—soon took a back seat with the onset of the Great Depression. By 1932, the excesses of the 1920s were but a memory.

The large number of automobiles sold was responsible for many of the new-found personal freedoms of the "Roaring Twenties." Auto repair shops sprang up all over Bay City, like Staudacher's Repair Shop. Pictured are (l to r) Otto Schroeder, Vincent Strak, and Mentor Staudacher.

New immigrants, more Catholics, and some minorities came into Bay City during the war years, and the community did not escape the prejudice of the 1920s. On the back of this photo is written: "Klan Rally, 1920; meeting held on West Side of Saginaw River—location generally known."

Streetcars and Interurbans

In 1889 the first electric streetcar made its run from the Third Street Bridge through West Bay City. S. O. Fisher, lumberman and politician, began the West Bay City Streetcar Company, and it soon ran along Salzburg and Marquette Avenues. By 1893 an electric line ran down Washington, Center, and Third streets in Bay City. All the lines eventually met at Center and Washington where a policeman inside an elevated kiosk directed traffic and transfers.

In 1895, the interurban, an all electric line, ran between Bay City, Saginaw, Flint, Detroit, and as far south as Cincinnati. The cars could approach speeds of 80 miles per hour and old-timers recall the trip between Bay City and Saginaw was faster by interurban than by the interstate highway. The automobile and jitney buses soon replaced both streetcars and interurbans. The electric streetcars were discontinued in 1921, and the interurban ran up until 1929.

Prior to the electric streetcar, horse-drawn cars ran as early as 1865. In 1882 a large car barn, pictured here, was built on Cass between Water Street and the river near the Astor House. The electric car first ran in West Bay City in 1889. Pictured here, to right of center, is Elizabeth Patterson Stokes and her family, 1885.

The Doran Bus Company was thought to be the city's first bus line beginning in 1922. It offered only one route from Patterson down Marquette on the West Side, and then across to Third Street to Center and Washington.

Early, open-air Bay City streetcar on a route to Wenona Beach. The fares to Wenona Beach were 15 cents round trip. This photo is probably 1895 or later, not, as noted, 1890.

173

Wenona Beach

Any Bay Citian born before 1950 likely remembers Wenona Beach, the beach resort north of town that provided many memories for the thousands who visited or vacationed there in the summer. Wenona Beach was probably the most popular resort south of Mackinac Island. For almost 80 years the park provided all classes with relaxation, entertainment, excitement, amusement, and music.

Wenona Beach actually was constructed by the old Bay City Street Car Co., in the late 1880s, in order to provide weekend and evening paying riders for the street railways. Free passes were often given out for roller-coaster or merry-go-round rides. For 15 cents visitors could make the 12-mile streetcar trip along Washington Street to Third Street, over the bridge to the West Side and then along Marquette before heading out on Patterson to the park. The fares kept the railway company profitable during the

Streetcar entrance to Wenona Beach. The amusement park was constructed by the Bay City Street Car Co. in the late 1880s to develop evening customers for its excursion cars. Electric cars ran every 10 minutes daily, and every 5 minutes on Sundays.

Postcard of the approach to the Casino, on left, at Wenona Beach. The Casino was built in 1903. On the right is Wright's Cafe which was later the Casino nightclub.

The Casino entrance. A large crowd awaits entrance prior to a vaudeville show in 1912. The Casino later became the Pier Ballroom. "Two high-class vaudeville acts daily," promised the Casino posters.

hard times after the lumber era.

The water on the beach was crystal clear and a two-block long boardwalk attracted visitors until 2 A. M. Children would ride on the roller-coaster (the Jackrabbit), the ferris wheel, or the old mill boat rides. All would visit Wright's Cafe for a five-course meal or picnic along the beach. In the evening the Pier Ballroom, and later the Beach Casino, were the night spots where big name bands—Guy Lombardo or Woody Herman—provided dance music into the morning hours. Wenona Beach was a haven for those who wanted to get away—if only for a day—from the cares of the Depression or later World War II. The automobile gave people greater mobility after the War, and television kept people at home. After Labor Day, 1964, the park was finally shut down for good. It lives on in postcard images, memories, faded pictures, and a picture book published in 1988 by Jim Watson.

Built just before World War I, the "Jackrabbit" was the all-time favorite ride. "It's probably condemned, but let's pray and go anyway." Everyone thought it would fall down on the next ride.

Dave Wright's Cafe. The highlight for many visitors to Wenona Beach was a five course meal at the cafe. Cream colored mints with sugared violets were served after each meal.

The interior of Wright's Cafe and Ice Cream Parlor. There was seating for 500 people when this photo was taken in 1904. After work at the cafe, the waitresses were allowed to go on all the rides for free.

Prohibition and Bay City Breweries

From before the days of the Catacombs' saloons, Bay Citians certainly enjoyed a drink or two after a hard day's work. Prohibition did not set well with a number of German, Polish, and Irish residents. Many were home brewers of beer as well as frequent visitors to one of the many restaurants or saloons.

By the time prohibition went into effect in Michigan in 1918, there were three large breweries producing beer in Bay City: Phoenix Brewing, Bay City Brewery, and the Kolb Brewery. All three stopped producing alcoholic beer in the 20s, but they

Bay City's breweries had flourished ever since the lumber heyday, but when Prohibition was enacted in Michigan in 1918, and the manufacture of alcoholic beer stopped, the three city breweries had to convert to other products like near beer, malt, and cereal beverages. All three breweries survived the Great Depression. By 1936, the breweries, like Bay City Brewery and Kolb Bros. were each producing up to 50,000 barrels a year of the "finest ale from Bay City water."

survived the Prohibition Era by producing malt, cereal beverages, and near beer. By the early 1950s, local breweries could not compete with national brands, and all were forced to close.

Speakeasys and blind pigs replaced saloons and breweries in the 1920s, and many Bay Citians continued to produce "home brew." Stills were common, especially in the rural areas, and many law-abiding citizens seemed to take delight in challenging a law which they considered an invasion of privacy. Malt was purchased from the breweries, alcohol was made in stills, a drop of glycerine, a little distilled water and a touch of juniper juice made a potent drink. "Anyone," it was said, "who couldn't get a drink wasn't trying."

During the Prohibition Era, Defoe Shipbuilding (above) converted its war production over to building Coast Guard Patrol Craft to pursue the rum-runners that delivered illegal beverages across the Detroit River.

Mr. M. Schindehette was an agent for Buckeye "Brewrey." Note the varied spelling for "brewery." His business was at 1300 Johnson Street.

The Kolb Bros. Beer Plant. Adam and George Kolb took over the business from their father in 1887. It was well known for its "Kolb Export Ale," and produced about 60,000 barrels annually before Prohibition. It was located on Germania Street on the West Side and manufactured beer there until the late 1930s.

Banks and the Great Depression

The first bank in Bay City was probably a wildcat bank built in 1838 by Judge Miller and James Fraser in the paper city of Lower Saginaw. After this, the first established bank was the Bay Bank opened in 1863. During the lumber era it was common for lumbermen to get together and establish their own financial institutions. In 1867 the First National Bank was chartered, which was the forerunner to Peoples National (now First of America). Judge Miller, Henry Sage, John McGraw, and W. L. Plum opened the Second National Bank on the West Side in 1874. In 1875, the Lumberman's State Bank was opened in West Bay City. In 1883, "Little Jake" Seligman, a popular Saginaw clothier and banker among the lumberjacks, opened a branch on Water Street. When the lumber business declined in the 1890s, a number of the city's banks were liquidated.

The stock market crash of 1929 presented a second financial crisis in Bay City banking. Many local banks had fueled the run-away prosperity of the 1920s by making cheap loans and taking real estate, stocks, or mortgages as collateral. When the collapse came, they could not sell their assets to pay off investors who needed cash. In September, 1931, the Bay City Bank shut down unable to pay its depositors. By December the First National also closed its doors. Only the Peoples Commercial and Savings Bank survived the Great Depression.

Interior of the Second National Bank, 1888. Inside the recently constructed Phoenix Building, the Second National claimed to "have the finest banking office in Michigan." In 1914, the Second National merged to form the Peoples Commercial Bank.

The Phoenix Building, built in 1887, housed the Second National Bank. In 1890, shipbuilder, Capt. James Davidson, became a board member and in 1902 was elected president. Three years later his son, James E. Davidson, was named president and became the city's foremost banker for several decades.

The First National Bank, Washington Avenue looking south from Center, in 1888. The Bank, which opened in 1864, was the first public bank in Bay City. It did not survive the Depression but managed to repay all depositors.

"DOLLAR FOR DOLLAR" HERO

After all of Bay City's banks had closed by December, 1931, a run was expected on the city's last open bank, Peoples Commercial. In order to prevent the city's financial collapse, bank president, James E. Davidson, the son of the shipyard owner, flew to Detroit from Clements Airport and came back with one million dollars in cash. He assured distraught depositors that he personally would guarantee their money "dollar for dollar." A few days later 50 Bay City merchants expressed confidence in Davidson's bank by lining up along Washington Avenue and parading, amid cheers, their funds into the bank. Soon afterward Davidson's bank loaned the city school board $80,000 to pay salaries and keep the schools open. Through his efforts, Davidson was able to restore confidence. By 1932 two new banks were opened and banking gradually returned to normal in Bay City.

The Peoples Commercial Bank was formed in 1914 through a merger of the Peoples Bank from the West Side, the Commercial Bank, and the Second National Bank. This photo was taken in 1949.

Movie Houses

Movies virtually took over Bay City during the Great Depression. Neighbors walked together or took the jitney bus to one of several local theaters. At the cost of a nickle, for a few hours they could escape the fears and concerns of unemployment, poverty, and later war.

The first motion pictures in Bay City were shown in the Washington Theater which replaced the old Woods Opera House after it burned down in 1902. Early on, Howe's Moving Pictures were shown to large audiences at the Washington. In 1908 the city directory reveals three theaters that combined movies and vaudevillian acts. By 1911 the number of theaters increased to 10 scattered throughout the city. Later on drive-in theaters in out-lying areas, and television stations began to cut into theater attendance. Several city theaters closed; however, in later years, they began to be replaced by modern, multiscreen complexes located in nearby malls.

The Bay City Symphony in concert at Washington Theater, 1931. Minnie B. Seymour, lst Violin, is in white, second row, third from left. Scores of prominent entertainers and bands played at the Washington for decades in the first half of the century including John Philip Sousa's band in 1913. Later on, the first St. Patrick's Day Queen in 1955 was selected on this stage.

The Woods Opera House, at Washington and Sixth, was opened in 1886 after the Westover Block burned that same year. It attracted almost every kind of performance including drama. opera, vaudeville, and high-school graduations. It was destroyed by fire in 1902. The Washington Theater reopened on the same site in 1903.

The Alvarado Theater at 521 Washington in 1911. Although there were only three movie houses in Bay City in 1908, by the time the Alvarado opened there were already eleven.

The Bijou Theater, 913 Washington, was both a vaudevillian theater and later a movie house.

Originally the Majestic, later the Crown, and eventually the Westown Theater, was located on Midland Street on the West Side. It was one of the last Bay City movie houses to close.

The Aladdin Theater, c. 1916, also once called the Alvarado and later the Center, was located at 716 Adams across from the old Penny's store.

181

CIRCUSES AND PARADES:

The first circus that played in Bay City was reportedly the Forepaugh Circus in 1864, at the corner of Woodside and Jefferson streets. Later the circuses moved to Trumbull and Seventh, the County Fairgrounds, and even the old Banks World War II housing site. The Ringling Bros. Circus played here four times around the turn of the century, and the Barnum and Bailey Circus came into town well into mid-century. In 1910, Buffalo Bill brought his "Wild West Show" to town with Indians, cowboys, and Buffalo Bill himself.

The circus parade attracted the crowds. As the circus came to town it moved its performers, elephants, clowns, lions, tigers, and monkeys along Center or Washington streets to the site of the big top. And like the rest of the nation, Bay City always had a love for a grand parade of any sort. From today's St, Patrick's Day Parade to old-time beer parades, political parades, victory parades and homecoming events, thousands turned out, and Bay City has seen them all.

Jack Davis, a former circus clown, became one of the most enthusiastic promoters for the circus and was also a well-known booster of Bay City. Here he is seen at the Beatty Show in 1979 with "Pete" the elephant.

Turn-of-the-century Fourth of July Parade. Note "Local and Long Distance Telephone" moving bell.

The entrance to the County Fairgrounds' Midway shows.

Elephants were marched down through the streets as part of the Circus Parade. The parade generated excitement and attendance at the circus. Here the elephants are about to march to the grounds in 1900.

Lions and tigers in cages were an important part of the parade as it traveled to the Fair Grounds in 1900.

Andrew Fisher and his Maxwell automobile are on their way to the Northeast Michigan Fair, c. 1922.

Bay City's finest at what appears to be an Odd Fellows parade. The famous actor Edwin Booth played at the newly opened Woods Opera House in the fall of 1886. Note placard.

Miss Eastern Michigan, 1931.

Miss Bay City, Agatha Ducharme, 1931.

Bay County Centennial Parade, June, 1957.

Bay City Parade down Washington Ave, c. 1890-1900.

185

WORLD WAR II

Shortly after the Japanese attack on Pearl Harbor in December, 1941, the entire manufacturing sector and Bay City's population mustered into the effort to defeat the Axis powers. Even before Pearl Harbor, the Red Arrow Division had been mobilized in October of 1940, and was later sent to Australia in April of 1942. From there, the Division was involved in 654 continuous days of combat in New Guinea and the Philippines against the Japanese. This was considered to be one of the longest periods in combat of any division during World War II. The Red Arrow Division won six medals of Honor and sustained 2,600 battlefield casualties. Hundreds of other young Bay City men and some women served in the European theater against the Germans.

The student body at the old Bay City Junior College fell from 400 to 75 students by 1943. If they hadn't enlisted in the Armed Services, most of the men and women were working in the nearby war-production factories. At home, war-time factory employment increased dramatically. Dow Chemical Company's magnesium operations grew to 3,300 employees as the demand for lightweight metal rapidly increased; Defoe shipbuilding had 4,000 workers laboring around the clock.

During the war Defoe shipbuilding organized its entire production to the war demands of the U. S. Government. In the four years Defoe built 154 ships including 54 Patrol Craft Vessels, minesweepers, submarine chasers, destroyer escorts, and landing craft. Thanks to the scale of shipbuilding, Defoe was a major contributor to the Allied effort to break the German submarine blockade on the north Atlantic routes. This enabled vast amounts of supplies to reach England in preparation for D-Day in 1944. It was also during the war years that Defoe developed the famous "rollover" type of construction. Welding was done much more quickly and enabled the company to build one PC craft every week.

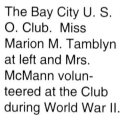

The Bay City U. S. O. Club. Miss Marion M. Tamblyn at left and Mrs. McMann volunteered at the Club during World War II.

Rosenbury & Sons Furniture store sponsored this patriotic newspaper advertisement during World War II.

The Defoe Shipyards in Bay City built 154 ships, including 54 "PC" boats, like the one seen in this photo, for the U. S. Navy during the war years.

On the homefront thousands of women left their homemaking jobs to help in the nearby war industries. Newspaper advertisements recruited both male and female workers, and after the war it was more acceptable for women to remain in the workforce. Even though the War Department tried to convince women to return home after the war in order to open job opportunities for returning veterans, the shape of the local work force changed forever. Women no longer worked just as babysitters, teachers, nurses or waitresses. They were now part of the permanent industrial labor force in Bay City.

The Second World War also created demands for new and temporary housing in Bay City. Emergency housing projects were built in the Banks area, in Washington Park, and on Fremont Avenue. Multi-family Quonset homes were quickly put up and they provided quarters not only for newcomers but for the returning veterans. Housing demands also created the first large-scale expansion to new homesites outside the city. All along Midland, Center, Euclid, and other main thoroughfares residential subdivisions were platted.

Prosperity after the war spurred the baby boom. Local school districts' enrollments increased dramatically and new schools were built. By a special election in 1949, the Board of Education passed a "Pay-as-you-Go," four-mill tax to cover school replacement over the next fifteen years. The new plan proposed four new elementary schools, several intermediate schools, and the expansion of Central and Handy high schools. The G. I. Bill enabled returning veterans to attend college, and Bay City Junior College's enrollment jumped to 750. Thousands of people were eager to settle for postwar prosperity within Bay City and its environs. Prosperity for all, especially within Bay City's newly industrialized economy, looked promising. A better life was on the horizon after 15 years of war and depression.

Herman Strevel, killed during the D-Day invasion at Normandy.

"Sunday Bond Buyer." Buy a bond and you can ride in the jeep! Floyd Ackerman, at typewriter, and Harold G. Bernstein sell war bonds in Bay City. Driver is R. L. Rimmer.

Bay City WAVE, Yeoman 3rd class, Ann Vukavich.

The Banks temporary housing units were put up in 1943 on the West Side industrial area to provide homes for the large number of factory workers needed in Bay City's industries during the war. They were being dismantled in this 1954 photo.

BAY CITY'S AVIATION PIONEERS

Shortly after the Wright brothers' initial flight, people in Bay City developed a keen interest in flying. As early as 1909 airplanes were being manufactured in Saginaw. Lionel H. DeRemer was probably the first Bay Citian to fly after he took flight instructions from the Wright School on Long Island, N. Y. Henry Dora, who was taught to fly by DeRemer, flew with Orville Wright at an air show in Saginaw. Their enthusiasm for flying was instrumental in the construction of James Clements Airport in 1929.

When she began to fly in 1932, Vera Janette Sovereign was Bay City's first female pilot. She won several air races and was the international president of "99" an organization of women pilots founded by Amelia Earhart.

Bay Citian, Lionel H. DeRemer, was the area's first pilot. He is shown, in center, with his "Wright B Pusher" equipped with pontoons bought from the Wright Bros. in 1912-13.

Below: James Clements Airport, c. 1940, opened in 1928 with Henry Dora as airport manager. Note WBCM airplane.

This American Eagle was flown by Bay City pilot Henry Dora in a raging snowstorm from St. Louis at 123 mph in 1928. Dora was an expert mechanic, early aviation pioneer and barnstormer in Bay City.

CHAPTER 8: DETERMINED DURABILITY

> *The world—and Bay City—is and will be different. We cannot resist or reverse the efforts of the basic economic and social forces of the market. And this is not all bad. In order to achieve this economic change Bay City needs strong social and cultural institutions that can bring us together across political and ethnic and class lines for shared experiences and shared causes.*
>
> **Eric R. Gilbertson, President,**
> **Saginaw Valley State University, 1996**

Perhaps there was no better time to absorb the spirit of Bay City than in the two decades following World War II. Tree-lined streets, comfortable and safe neighborhoods; jobs at Chevy, IB, Prestolite, or Defoe; and parks and old buildings were there for all to enjoy. Postwar prosperity also brought runaway inflation, and the demand for increased wages contributed to labor difficulties that further alienated worker from employer in Bay City. But all of these changes occurred slowly, and few would deny that these were perhaps some of the last fine times that Bay City enjoyed prior to the economic upheavals of the 1970s and 80s.

Factors that affected the entire nation and region had a significant impact on Bay City. The oil crisis of the 1970s and the restructuring of the auto business forced Bay City manufacturers to close aging production facilities. Defoe Shipbuilding, Industrial Brownhoist, and Prestolite closed down operations in these two decades and put thousands out of work. A declining tax base and new demands for services plagued the city's and school board's finances. Bay City was now part of the so-called "rust-belt." By 1990, the U. S. Census reported that the city population had fallen below 40,000 people.

Nonetheless, Bay City is a durable city. It has fought with determination—albeit with mixed results—to redefine itself in the post-industrial era.

Bay City was an exciting, prosperous, and comfortable place to live in the post-World War II era. This is a view after the war south down Washington Avenue from Center. Note the old Sears on right and Washington Theater on the left.

Its economy has successfully been transformed in the last decade into a more diverse mix than perhaps at any time in its history. True, often the new jobs are not the well-paying industrial jobs of the past, but few cities in the country can count on a dependable, industrial economy for their stability. Unemployment is relatively low in Bay City and many small- and medium-sized companies are moving into the county.

The quality of life in Bay City has again reaffirmed itself. It is a community with a viable downtown, little crime, and a flourishing recreational and entertainment industry. A strong sense of history and pride in its past accomplishments and institutions prevails. Sometimes this sense of history slows change and creates divisiveness. Leaders are sometimes frustrated by the determination to preserve the past. But at the same time it is this determined durability that has moved Bay City successfully toward the twenty-first century.

What is still needed is a grand effort to overcome some of those legacies of the past that have been seen in this Logbook; especially those legacies that have created separate societies and different interests. At the end of the twentieth century it should be clear that historically Bay Citians have much in common. They share cultural diversity, a common river and bay, a liveable community, and a strong sense of family and place. These resources should be enough to continue to build upon well into the new century.

Post-War prosperity and the baby boom brought rapid residential growth to Bay City and the surrounding communities in the 1950s. Seventy-five percent of Bay City's residents were home owners when this photo of a new subdivision was taken in 1950.

Center Avenue looking west from Washington Avenue in the late 1960s.

The right to drive for Bay City teens in the 1960s often meant the right to drive to Richies Drive-In on Euclid Avenue. "French fries, a coke and hamburger, that's all!"

"It's a Downright Lonesome Feeling, the Passing of the Train."

The years after World War II witnessed the passing of the passenger trains. In 1915 Bay City was considered one of eastern Michigan's railroading centers with 31 passenger trains arriving and departing the city each day. Repair shops, round houses, regional offices, and several beautiful railroad stations made Bay City a railroad hub. The city had, a decade earlier, closed off Fourth between Adams and Madison streets for construction of the grand Pere Marquette station. By the start of World War I, Bay City served as headquarters for three divisions of the Michigan Central and the short-lived Detroit, Bay City and Western. The city was also served by the Detroit and Mackinac, the Pere Marquette, and the Grand Trunk.

The Detroit and Mackinac Railroad was reorganized in 1894 from the remnants of several earlier lumber lines that served the eastern part of the state from Bay City to Alpena. The D & M continued to grow, and in 1946 all of its steam locomotives were replaced by diesel-driven engines. However, because of the automobile, the D & M abandoned passenger service entirely in 1951. No longer were passengers taking the train on those memorable summer resort excursions to the D & M's popular resort grounds at Tawas or Linwood Beach.

The Handy brothers built the 108 mile, Detroit, Bay City and Western line in 1911 to serve the agricultural communities in the thumb. The railroad chugged back and forth between Port Huron and Bay City from 1911 to 1925. Excursions ran from the thumb into Bay City inviting farmers and their families to local circuses or fairs. Eight coaches, each seating 70 persons, were often filled on the D. B. C. & W.'s four daily passenger trips. The Handy line also had two freight trains daily that hauled beets, grain, hay, lumber, and coal into Bay City. This railroad ran into

Robert B. Ketchum was the engineer and seventy years old when this photo was taken in front of the New York Central's Steam Locomotive, Engine 8371, in Bay City on December 1, 1926.

Detroit, Bay City and Western Railroad cars and engine. The line operated between Bay City and Port Huron between 1911 and 1925.

financial trouble in the mid-1920s and closed down.

Passenger train service began to dwindle and disappear from Bay City in mid-century. The D & M stopped its run between Bay City and Alpena in 1951; and the Chesapeake and Ohio discontinued the run between Saginaw and Bay City in 1949. Grand Trunk passenger trains that ran from Bay City to Durand, stopped carrying passengers in 1958, and GT also closed its Midland Street station. The last passenger train, the New York Central, "Beeliner," ran from Bay City to Detroit until 1964. Times reporter, David Miller, remembered this last ride past "a million memories and long ribbons of super highways," that contributed to the end of the passenger train to Bay City.

The Pere Marquette Railroad Depot in downtown Bay City, between Adams and Jefferson, still stands as a landmark to the memories of the grand days of railroading travel.

The old Michigan Central Station was a grand structure and served the northern area of the city. The station was located at First and Jackson streets. Standing abandoned here, it burned twice and was torn down after the second fire in 1964.

The Salzburg Station in West Bay City.

South Bay City was served by its own Depot in the 1890s. The depot was the Flint & Pere Marquette's and on Jennison and South Center streets.

The last run of steam locomotives out of Bay City. The New York Central, January 1, 1956. On the left is Engine 7538, and Engine 2040, and in the rear is the new diesel engine coming out of the Bay City roundhouse yards.

C & O deisel Engine 97 at the Pere Marquette station in downtown Bay City.

OUR HIGH SCHOOLS

Over the years many changes have occurred in the structure of Bay City's schools. Probably the two most significant have been the steady, but gradual consolidation of the smaller district school systems into a few large units. At one time there were over 60 separate districts in the county. The second change was a result of the political consolidation of Bay City and West Bay City. For decades the Board of Education has tried to maintain a delicate balance of equal educational opportunities for the people on both sides of the river. This at times produced intense and rancorous debate over the closing and consolidation of elementary, middle, and even high schools. But it has also engendered spirited rivalries that have carried over into high school athletics. The annual Central versus Handy football game or basketball contests created enthusiasm and school spirit that existed for days before and after each event.

In 1868 West Bay City opened Center School at Wenona and John streets, a combined grade and high school, that soon became West Bay City High. A year later Farragut, also a combined school at Grant and Ninth Streets, was built and became the first Bay City High School. A new Bay City High School was built in 1882 at Madison near Columbus and became Eastern High School. Two separate high schools on each side of the river remained until 1922 when Bay City Central was built, and the old West Bay City High closed. Bay City Handy was also opened in 1922 as a junior high school. In 1948 Handy was converted into a high school and, once more, East and West Siders engaged in fierce cross-town athletic rivalries.

Consolidation of rural districts within Bay City and population growth west of town compelled the system to open a third high school in Auburn in 1973. However, by the 1980s, the loss of the industrial populations, a subsequent shrinking tax base, and the failure of several millage elections compelled the Board to consider reconverting Handy to a junior high school. This was done amid much West Side opposition in 1990. Today Bay City is once again served by two, east-west high schools, although to many the athletic rivalries of the past are no longer carried on with the same fervor that once characterized every Central-Handy clash.

Bay City Central High School, photographed here in 1937, was opened in 1922 and served students from both the East and West Sides until 1948.

Bay City Handy, originally a junior high school, became the West Side high school in 1948. Several additions were made to the school over the years.

PAROCHIAL SCHOOLS

Bay City's large Catholic and Lutheran populations insured the creation of many sectarian schools in order to instill religious instruction within its youth. St. James High School, which opened in 1873, was widely acclaimed as the nation's first coeducational Catholic high school. Many of the Catholic parishes had grade or high schools. Most of the high schools eventually consolidated into All Saints when it opened in 1968. The Lutheran Churches, both the Wisconsin and Missouri synods, operated a number of parochial grade schools in the county-wide area.

COLLEGES

The Devlin Business College, or the Northeastern School of Commerce was the first institution of higher learning in Bay County, opening in 1880. Bay City Junior College, the state's third junior college, opened in 1922 and held classes in the new Bay City Central High School. There was a teacher's college, Bay County Normal, that met in the old Riegel School until it consolidated with the junior college in 1954. Delta College evolved out of a tri-county effort to create a centrally located college to serve the entire Saginaw Valley. A local college tax base was established by the voters of Bay, Midland, and Saginaw counties, and Delta opened in 1961.

Top: T. L. Handy High School, Homecoming, 1956. Queen Sue Wuepper is presented at halftime.

Left: Old Bay City Western High School's Orchestra in 1920. Two years later the school closed and West Side students attended Central High.

Bottom left: Handy High school cheerleaders, 1963: Left to right, Jan Niedzielski, Cindy Jones, Jan Lamson, Kathy Forgash, Mona Shark.

Bottom right: Central's cheerleaders, 1957-58: Left to right, Sue Bradner, Nancy Cunningham, Janet Cunningham, Sue Dachlein, Elena Fulton.

HIGH SCHOOL SPORTS

Bay City Handy's Class A, State Champion Football team, 1961. Head coach, H. Becker (center, back row) guided the Wildcats to the State and Valley titles with a 8-0 record.

Coach Elmer Engel was perhaps Bay City's most well-known sports figure by the 1970s. In 23 years he guided Bay City Central's Wolves to five state championships and was considered the most successful coach in Michigan prep history. He captured four state crowns in eight years between 1965 and 1972. Here he stands with senior Paul Johnson who won All-American prep honors on Engel's 1964 team.

Coach Engel's 1972, Class A State Champions had a perfect 9-0 record.

All Saints

All Saints Homecoming Queen, 1975. Diane Kaunitz stands with her court.

Coach Russell "Lefty" Franz led the Cougars to their first back-to-back state championship titles in 1974-75. Coach Franz won a total of 545 basketball victories and was enshrined in the Michigan High School Coaches Hall of Fame.

Mark Talaga scores an easy two points for the 1974 Class C Champions. Talaga broke the school scoring record that year.

1975 State Champs. Back row: Gary Socia, Jim Dominowski, Greg Heme, Jim Walsh, Tim Trepkowski, Joe Sasiela, Coach Franz. Front row: Gary Rasdorf, Craig Learman, Bill Harris, Wayne Sevilla, Ron Morse, Mike Nutt, Mark Holka.

Park School's 1906 City Championship Team with mascot

"The Chief," Coach Garland Nevitt, coached at Central High through the 1920s and developed several championship teams. Here he poses with his 1926 Central High basketball team. The 1926 team had a 7-7 record and averaged 11.5 points per game.

Western High School's 1913 girls basketball squad. Western was a Class A high school and competed in the Saginaw Valley Conference beginning in 1904.

SPORTS NOTABLES

Mark Jaffe was probably the best tennis player to come out of Bay City. He played three years at the University of Michigan and guided the Wolverines to an NCAA championship in 1975. He was a consistent winner of several state tennis championships later in his career.

Art Bakeraitis could have been a pro in baseball, basketball, or football. He was a three-sport letterman at Central and when he graduated in 1943 was offered professional baseball and football contracts. Instead he signed with the Detroit Vagabond Kings pro basketball team.

Dennis Wirgowski was a high school All-American at Bay City Central in football. He later played defensive end at Purdue and five seasons in the NFL. He is often considered Bay City's most outstanding prep football player.

Hazen "Ki-Ki" Cuyler was born in Harrisville, but began his professional baseball career in Bay City. He played 18 years in the National League from 1921-38, and was an outstanding outfielder for the Pittsburgh Pirates on the 1925 World Series Championship team. He was later inducted into the Baseball Hall of Fame.

Jerry Gross was often considered too small for football, but as Central's quarterback he was good enough to land a scholarship to the University of Detroit. There he became first team Catholic All-American in 1962 and broke several passing records in the 1962 Senior Bowl.

Bill Hewitt played at Central and the U of M, but really made his name as an 11-year pro football player. "Stinky" Hewitt guided the Chicago Bears to two world championships between 1932 and '36. He was killed in an auto accident in 1947 at the age of 37.

Bay City Legends

Bay City school teacher Ann Edson Taylor who rode over the Horseshoe Falls at Niagara in 1901 in a wooden barrel was the first person to ride over the falls in a barrel and live. She climbed out of the barrel with only a gash and a slight concussion. Although, well-spoken and educated, Mrs. Taylor was never able to turn her stunt into a profitable venture. She died in 1921 and was buried in a pauper's grave at Niagara Falls, N. Y.

Terry McDermott, from Essexville, won the gold medal in the 1964 Winter Olympics, and took the silver medal in 1968. McDermott, a Bay City barber at the time, experienced one of the largest welcome home receptions and parades ever given in Bay City. He is pictured here with Fr. McHugh and Fr. Hietpass from St. John's in Essexville from where he graduated.

Les Staudacher, the Kawkawlin power-boat builder, built perhaps more Gold Cup hydroplanes than any other boat builder. Some of Staudacher's boats have hit speeds of 250 mph. He built several *Tempo* boats for band leader and racer Guy Lombardo. He also built the "Miss Pepsi" series and the *Gale* boats. Together these and others won 30 Gold Cup races.

Fabian Joe Fournier was a legendary lumberjack and well-known Bay City brawler who lived in the Banks area. D. Laurence Rogers, past editor of the *Bay City Times*, wrote a book in which he claims Fournier's exploits inspired the Paul Bunyan legends. Fournier was clubbed to death by a gang of shanty boys and one Blinky Robinson after a fight on the corner of Third and Water streets in 1875. Reportedly his skull was used as evidence, and because of its double row of teeth, put on display for years at the County Courthouse.

Elaine Baker was the daughter of Oscar W. Baker, the city's first black attorney. Elaine studied vocal arts at Central High and majored in voice at MSU. She continued her studies in New York and soon became an established opera singer. She performed throughout Europe and the U.S. and lived in Munich Germany. In 1954 she won the American Theatre award and continued to sing and teach for years in Germany and throughout Europe.

Legend Check — WHAT DID MADONNA REALLY SAY?

Madonna Louise Ciccone is probably Bay City's most famous native. While she never lived in Bay City, Madonna was born at Mercy Hospital on August 16, 1958. Her mother, also named Madonna, had moved to the Pontiac area, but returned to her hometown to have the family doctor deliver her third child. While the singer and actress grew up in Rochester, MI., often, as a young girl, she returned to stay with her maternal grandmother on Smith Street in the Banks area. Madonna never lived here longer then a few months during summer vacations and never attended Bay City's schools.

Because of her appearance in *Playboy* and *Penthouse* magazines in 1985, the mayor of Bay City refused to offer Madonna the key to the city.

In 1987 Madonna caused considerable commotion in Bay City when, on the Today Show, she referred to her birthplace as "a smelly little town in northern Michigan." A week later, during a concert at the Pontiac Silverdome, Madonna publicly apologized for the slight: "I didn't mean the people of Bay City stink, just the Dow Chemical plant," she said. She went on to say that she did not want to be the cause of a lot of commotion "in the city where I was born. I'd better keep my mouth shut now."

In 1988, Bay City also refused to accept an Italian sculptor's 13-foot statue of the pop star. The mayor and city manager did not think Bay City would be an appropriate home for the art piece.

CITY LIFE ALONG THE RIVER: THE FUTURE!

Bay City's most important resources are the Saginaw River and Saginaw Bay. The river has been a lifeline for commerce, industry, and recreation for nearly two centuries. At the end of the twentieth century a good deal of attention is being focused on efforts to revitalize the riverfront and create an attractive environment for tourists. The river walk, rail-trail and rowing club are good examples of using the river first and foremost for the residents of Bay City and not simply to attract the ephemeral tourist dollar.

River restoration should be pursued simply to enhance the quality of life for Bay County residents. Imagine a river lined with parks, small businesses, restaurants, condominiums, large single-family houses, and affordable homes within walking distance of shops, schools, trails and the bay. To accomplish this, urban sprawl should be discouraged, re-configuration of riverfront properties pursued with energy, and the entire Saginaw Valley watershed monitored to improve the river's quality. Provide a picturesque waterway and they will come. Small manufacturers, light industries, and new residents would provide the stable economy that Bay City has been seeking for the past 100 years.

The Saginaw River running through Bay City toward Saginaw Bay. Although considerable river-front changes have occurred since this mid-century photograph, Bay City continues to struggle with the remnants of the old industrial buildings scattered along the urban riverfront.

Aerial view of Bay City for Centennial Souvenir Program, 1857-1957.

Acknowledgements

The rich history of Bay City is in large part preserved in the files and photographic collections of the Bay County Historical Society. Without the support of Director, Gay McInerney, as well as the staff at the museum, this publication would not have been possible. The Society allowed archivist Ronald Bloomfield to work directly on this project. Ron took an active part in not only discovering photographs, but proofread the text, and aided in content selection and layout. Likewise we are grateful to Citizens Bank of Bay City for their support and promotion of this undertaking. A special thanks is also extended to those who made photographs available and complied with the sometimes urgent requests of the author.

The special assistance of several individual volunteers at the Historical Society cannot go unmentioned. Lois Honsowetz used her well-honed skills as a teacher and editor to proofread the entire text several times. For her time, commitment, and invaluable suggestions we are grateful beyond words. Emeritus professor of history at Delta College, Patricia Drury, passed on to us the edited writings of Myra Parsons that illuminate much to our text. Ron Putz allowed us to rummage through his photo collection and discover several noteworthy, unpublished photographs.

Thanks also to to several others who made special efforts to find photographs: Naomi Weber, Irma Guzman and the Guadalupe Center, and Duff Zube. We were also most fortunate to have John McCormick from Delta College and Bay City, well-known for his automobile paintings and other historic panoramas, illustrate the original cover. Our appreciation is also extended to publisher Brad Baraks for his efforts and time in advising in the selection of photos.

Lastly, we both would like to thank our wives and families for their time, patience, and sustained support on this project.

J. W. K.
R. W. B.

Contributors

Michele Allen	Kim Davis	Nola Johnson	Charles Pawlek	Dale Wolicki
Virginia Bell	William Ewald	Annalisa Kilar	Ronald Putz	Duff Zube
Rick Burn	Mike Fogelsinger	Stephen W. Kilar	Carol Sharp	
Paul Cameron	Maureen Graff	William Mayhew Jr.	Karen Sharp	
Barry A. Carlson	Brian Grew	Rodney McEachern	Ted Swift	
William T. Clynes	Irma Guzman	Ruth Neitzel	Naomi Weber	

Bibliography & Bay City Historians

Allen, Clifford and Harold Titus, eds. *Michigan Log Marks.* East Lansing: Michigan State College, 1941.

Arndt, Les. *By These Waters.* Bay City: The Bay City Times, 1976.

_____. *The Bay County Story: From Footpaths to Freeways.* Detroit: Harlo Printing, 1982.

Baker, Catherine C. *Shipbuilding on the Saginaw.* Bay City: Museum of The Great Lakes, 1974.

_____. *Vanished Industries of Bay County.* Bay City: Museum of The Great Lakes, 1980.

Bay City Times, Centennial Edition, June 16, 1957.

Barondes, Margaret M. "Backhoes, Bulldozers, and Behemoths." *Michigan History* 80 (Jan.-Feb., 1996).

Brown, David. "Restoring the Trombley-Center House." *Michigan History* 69 (May-June, 1985).

Butterfield, George E. *Bay County Past and Present.* Bay City: Board of Education, 1957.

Catton, Bruce. *Michigan: A History.* New York: Norton Company, 1976.

Colloway, Colin G. "The End of an Era: British-Indian Relations in the Great Lakes Region After the War of 1812." *Michigan Historical Review* 12 (Fall, 1986), 1-20.

Conlin, Joseph. "Food in the Logging Camps." *Encyclopedia of Forest and Conservation History.* Vol I. New York: McMillian Co., 1983.

Defebaugh, James E. *History of the Lumber Industry of America.* Chicago: American Lumberman, 1906.

Dow, H. S. *The History and Commercial Advantages, and Future Prospects of Bay City, Michigan.* Bay City: n. p., 1875.

Dustin, Fred. "The Treaty of Saginaw, 1819." *Michigan History* 4 (1920), 19-22.

Elliot, Frank N. *When the Railroad Was King: The Nineteenth Century Railroad Era in Michigan.* Lansing: Michigan Department of State. 1977.

Fitting, James E. *The Archaeology of Michigan.* Bloomfield Hills: Cranbrook Institute of Science, 1975.

Fitzmaurice, John. *The Shanty Boy or Life in a Lumber Camp.* Reprint of 1889 edition. Ann Arbor: Historical Society of Michigan, 1978.

Frazier, Jean. *Ka-wam-da-meh: A Study of Michigan's Major Indian Tribes.* Grand Ledge: Herman E. Cameron Foundation, 1989.

Gansser, Augustus H. *History of Bay County, Michigan and Representative Citizens.* Chicago: Richmond and Arnold, 1905.

Goodstein, Anita Shafer. *Biography of a Businessman: Henry W. Sage, 1814-1897.* Ithaca, N. Y.: Cornell University Press, 1962.

Greenman, Emerson F. "The Indians of Michigan." *Michigan History* 43 (March, 1961); 1-34.

Gross, Stuart D. *Saginaw: A History of the Land and the City.* Woodland Hills, Calif.: Windsor Publications, 1980.

Halsey, John R. "The Wayne Mortuary Complex." *Michigan History* 65 (Sept.-Oct. 1981).

Augustus Gansser not only saw service in the Spanish-American War and World War I, but later wrote a history of Bay City's 33rd and 34th Michigan Infantry Divisions. In 1908 he wrote the honest and extremely insightful *History of Bay County.* It remains an essential resource for anyone assessing Bay City right after its lumber era prosperity. Gansser became a member of the Michigan State House of Representatives from Bay County in 1911, and was a state Senator from 1915 to 1933.

George E. Butterfield was actively involved in Bay City's public education system and was a long-time President of the Bay County Historical Society. Former principal of several schools, it was as Dean Emeritus of Bay City Junior College that Mr. Butterfield undertook the publication of *Bay County Past and Present* in the county centennial year, 1957. The history remains the standard introductory text to Bay County's past. He and especially his son, Ira W. Butterfield, were also involved in local Native American archaeology George Butterfield died in 1975.

Hargraves, Irene M., and Harold M. Foehl. *Logging the White Pine.* Bay City: Red Keg Press, 1964.

History of Bay County, Michigan. Chicago: H. R. Page & Co., 1883.

Hinsdale, W. R. *Distribution of Aboriginal Populations of Michigan.* Ann Arbor: Museum of Anthropology, University of Michigan, 1932.

Holbrook, Stewart H. *Holy Old Mackinaw.* New York: Macmillian and Co., 1938.

Hotchkiss, George W. *History of the Lumber and Forest Industry of the Northwest.* Chicago: G. W. Hotchkiss & Co., 1898.

Kilar, Jeremy W. "A Comparative Study of Lumber Barons as Community Leaders in Saginaw, Muskegon, and Bay City." *Michigan History* 74 (July-August, 1990), 35-42.

_____. "Black Pioneers in the Michigan Lumber Industry." *Journal of Forest History* 24 (July, 1980), 13-19.

_____. "Community and Authority Response to the Saginaw Valley Lumber Strike., 1885." *Journal of Forest History,* 24 (April, 1976), 67-79.

_____. "Law and Order in Lumber Camps and Towns." *Encyclopedia of Forest and Conservation History,* Vol I. New York: MacMillian and Co., 1983.

_____. *Michigan's Lumbertowns: Lumbermen and Laborers in Saginaw, Bay City and Muskegon, 1870-1905.* Detroit: Wayne State University Press, 1990.

_____. *Saginaw's Changeable Past: An Illustrated History.* St. Louis, MO. G. Bradley Publishing, 1994.

_____. "Tocqueville's Companion Traveler: Gustave de Beaumont and the Journey into the Michigan Wilderness in 1831." *Michigan History* 68 (Jan.-Feb., 1984), 34-39.

Mainfort, Robert C., Jr. *Indian Social Dynamics in the Period of European Contact: Fletcher Site Cemetery.* East Lansing: Michigan State University Museum, 1979.

Maybe, Rolland H. *Michigan's White Pine Era, 1840-1900.* Lansing: Michigan Historical Commission, 1960.

McClurken, James E. "Ottawa Adaptive Strategies to Indian Removal." *Michigan Historical Review* 12 (Spring, 1986), 29-56.

McCormick, William. *Pioneer Memories.* Bay City: Bay County Historical Society, 1995.

Meek, Forest. *Michigan's Timber Battleground.* Clare, MI.: n. p., 1976.

Moll, Harold W. "A Canoe Trip to Midland, Michigan in 1675." *Michigan History* 46 (Fall, 1962), 255-76.

Reimann, Lewis R. *When Pine Was King.* Autrain, MI.: Avery Color Studio, 1981.

Rogers, David L. *Paul Bunyan: How a Terrible Timber Feller Became a Legend.* Bay City: Historical Press, 1993.

Smith, Bradley and Jeremy W. Kilar. *Tobico Marsh: The Story of the Land and the People.* Bay City: Jennison Nature Center, 1987.

Tanner, Helen H. *Atlas of Great Lakes Indian History.* Chicago: Newberry Library, and Norman: The University of Oklahoma Press, 1986.

Vanderhill, Warren C. *Settling the Great Lakes Frontier: Immigration to Michigan, 1837-1924.* Lansing: Michigan Historical Commission, 1970.

Wakefield, Francis. "The Elusive Mascoutens," *Michigan History* 50 (September, 1966), 228-234.

Catherine Baker was a collector and an author. She and her husband amassed a large local history library and put it to good use. She wrote several introductory books for the County Historical Society on topics such as shipbuilding in Bay City and pioneer Bay City industries. Mrs. Baker was also the local correspondent for the *Detroit Free Press.* Cathy and Paul Baker ran Baker's Yacht Service in Essexville for many years and willingly shared their local history discoveries with all who shared their interests.

Leslie E. Arndt was a long-time staff writer for the *Bay City Times.* His historical columns in the *Times* became the basis for several insightful and thorough books on Bay City's past. *By These Waters,* and later in 1982 his quasquicentennial book, *The Bay County Story; From Footpaths to Freeways* have become sought-after collector's items. Les was also the founder of Bay City's first People-to-People chapter in 1966, and a long-time favorite for his reenactments of Davy Crockett.

Index

A
Absentee Ownership 85, 95
Ackerman, Floyd 187
African-Americans 95, 110
Agriculture 112
Aladdin Homes 147
Allardt, Max 102
Aldelphi Theater 56
Alger, Russel A. 95
Amelith School 123
American Fur Company 159
Anderson, Fred 159
Anishnabeg Indians 16-18
Arbeiter Hall 103
Archaic Indian Culture 12-13, 17
Armory, Michigan National Guard 157, 168-69
Arnold & Catlin 47
Arndt, Leslie E. 205
Astor, John Jacob 20
Auburn 116
Au Gres 44
Auto-Lite 148, 151
Aviation 188

B
Baker, Catherine 295
Baker, Elaine 201
Baker, James H. 110
Baker, Oscar W. 110
Bakeraitis, Art 199
Banks, The 30, 52, 58-59
Banks in Bay City 178-79
Barry, Thomas 95
Baseball Teams 165
Bay City Cash Dry Goods Store 140
Bay City, City Hall 156
Bay City Dredge Works 91, 132-34
Bay City Flouring Mills 141
Bay City:
  Growth and Settlement 34, 58-59
  Immigrant Populations 96-97
  Junior College 186-87, 195
  Logging Era 39-44
  Organized 29
  Neighborhoods 39, 68
  Populations 10 28-29, 39, 166, 189
  Railroads 54-56
  Subscription Hospitals 78
  Unfication 155
  Waterfront 202
  Violence in 70
Bay County
  Archaeology 11, 19
  Centennial, 1957 185
  Infirmary 79
  Jail 70

Bay County Building 155
Becker, H. 196
Beaumont, Gustave de 18, 23
Beavers and Trapping 21
Belgians 93, 107
Bernstein, Harold G. 187
Big Wheels 43
Bigelow and Cooper Salt 45
Bird, Andrew 120
Birney, James G. 27-29, 44
Birney, James G., Jr. 54-55
Blair, Gov. Austin 82
Boardinghouses 65
Board of Education 187
Board of Trade 138
Bois Mill 46
Booming 44
Booth, Edwin 184
Bousfield, A. S. 98
Bousfield Woodenware 46-47
Boutell, Arnold 90
Boutell, Capt. Benjamin 51
Boutell Farm 112
Bradley, Nathan B. 78, 90, 119
Breen's Bicycle Shop 144
Breweries 176-77
Bridges 160
Brooks, Kate 110
Bull Moose Party, (1912) 187
Burkhardt's Market 103
Butterfield, George 18, 19, 204
Butterfield, Ira 19, 204

C
Campau, Louis 20, 22
Carnegie Libraries 81
Cass, Gov. Lewis 21-22
Catacombs 56, 59, 60, 65
Catton, Bruce 35
Cemeteries 127
Center Ave. 61, 190
Center Ave. Residences 60-61
Center House 19, 23, 17, 29, 30
Chamberlain, Joshua 83
Cheboyganing Creek 18, 19, 162
Chevrolet Motor Division 148-49
Chippewa Indians 15-19
Churches:
  Evangelical Free 106
  First Baptist 118
  First Congregationalist 118
  First Presbyterian 117
  First Methodist 117
  Grace Episcopal 117
  Holy Trinity 103
  Jewish Temple 109
  Lutheran Churches 33
  Messiah Lutheran 106
  Our Lady of Guadalupe 111

  Second Baptist 110
  St. Anne's Linwood 99
  St. Boniface 103, 119
  St. Hyacinth 101
  St. Hedwig 101
  St. James 108
  St. John the Evangelist 107
  St. Mary's 108
  St. Paul's Lutheran 103
  St. Stanislaus 101, 119
  St. Valentine 101
  Trinity Episcopal 118
  Visitation 99
  Zion Lutheran 119
Child Labor 92-94
Ciccone, Madonna Louise 201
Circuses 182-83
Civil War 82-83
Civil War, G.A.R. 82-83
Clements, William L. 81
Coal Minning 133-34
Cook, Edward J. 75
Constineau, Victor 170
Craemer, August 33
Crime and Violence 70
Crosthwaite, William 48
Crump, Susie M. 122
Curtis, Charles B. 91
Cuyler, Hazen "Ki-Ki" 199

D
Danielewski, Ludwig 100-01, 119
Davidson, Capt. James 48-49
Davidson, James E. 178-79
Davis, Jack 135
Defoe, Harry J. 135
Defoe Shipbuilding 135, 177, 185-86
Delta College 195, 69
DeRemer, Lionel H. 188
Detroit, Bay City and Western RR 191
Detroit and Mackinac RR 191
Devlin Business College 195
Dolsen, Chapin & Company 61
Dolsenville 32
Dolsenville Salt Works 45
Dora, Henry 188
Doran Bus Company 173
Dow, Alden 109
Dow Chemical Company 149-151
Ducharme, Agatha 185
Durant, William C. 149
Dutch 93, 107

E
Eastern High School 164
Elliot's Blacksmith Shop 24-29
Engel, Elmer 196

Essexville 107
Ethnic Neighborhoods 96-111

F
Fairfax, Daniel 120
Farmer's Market 154
Fay, W. C., 90
Fire Companies 74
Fire Departments 73
Firehouses 74-76
Fires in Bay City 77-79
Fisher, Andrew 183
Fisher, S. O. 87, 193
Fishing 32, 52-53
Fitzhugh, Daniel H. 28-29, 30, 44, 119
Fitzhugh, Daniel, Jr. 29
Fletcher Site 19
Flint and Pere Marquette RR 197
Floods 162
Flu Epidemic (1918) 168
Folsom, Alexander 90
Fort Ponchartrain 16-17
Fort Saginaw 23
Fournier, Fabian Joc 201
Frankenmuth 33
Fraternal Societies 128-29
Frantz, C. H. 145
Franz, Russell "Lefty" 197
Fraser, James 26, 28, 58
Fraser, James I. 90
Freeman, H. C. 123
French Canadians 30, 32, 93-99
Frenchtown 32
Fur Trade 20-21
Funerals 126-27

G
Galarno's General Store 60
Gansser, Augustus 84, 167-68, 170, 204
Germans 30, 61, 83, 93, 95, 102-04
  in Strike of 1885 95
  in World War I 169
Gilbertson, Eric R. 189
Goddeyne, Joseph 185
Grand Trunk RR 191
Graveradt, Jacob 20
Great Lakes Shipping 50-51
Gross, Jerry 199

H
Hall, J. R., Sawmill 16, 46
Harman & Verner 152-53
Henry, Hi 150
Hell's Half Mile 64
Hewitt, Bill 199
Hispanic Settlers 111

Hitchcock & Bialy Mill 42
Hopewell Indians 11-13
Home Birth 80
Homicides in Bay City 70
Hospitals 78-79
Housewares Industry 164
Housing Industry 147
Housing in World War II 187, 190
Hotels 63-69
  Astor House 66
  Bay Shore 67
  Forest City 65
  Franklin House 66
  Fraser House 29, 65, 77
  Globe 28-29
  Lefevre 68
  Maple Grove 66
  New Clifton 68
  Portland House 65
  Republic 65, 67
  Smith's European 68
  Wolverton House 29, 65
  Wenonah 69, 77
Hyatt, W. S. Funeral Home 127

I
Independent Order of Odd Fellows 29
Indian Villages (Map) 11
Industrial Brownhoist 132, 189
Ingers and LaRoche 99
Interurban 173
Interurban, Disaster (1897) 162
Irish 61, 93, 108
Iroquois Wars 18
Ittner's Corner (Willard) 115

J
Jackson, Lansing & Saginaw RR 55
Jaffe, Mark 199
James Clements Airport 188
Jennison Hardware 140
Jerome, Gov. David 82
Jewish Settlers 109
Johnson, Paul 196
Johnson, Swan 139
Jones Clinic 79

K
Kaczynski Family 100
Kahn, Alex 109
Kantzler Lumber Yard 97
Kawkawlin 19
Kawkawlin River 130, 160
Ketchum, Robert B. 191
Kindekins, Fr. Joseph 107
King, Charles 170

206

Kiwanis Club 129
Kneeland-Bigelow 92
Knepps Department Store 138
Koch, Frederick 33
Kowalski Family 97
Kramer Family 103
Kresge, S S., Store 1452
Kuhlman Electric 148
Ku Klux Klan 172

L
Labor 85, 92-94
  Women 94
  Strikes 95
Lady Macabees 129
Landon, Dr, Henry 82
Law Enforcement 71-73
Lentz, A., Boots and Shoes 142
Lewis Built Homes 147
Liberty Homes 147
Libraries 81
List, J. F., Grocery 143
Logging 34-38
  Camplife 36-38
  Seasonal Occupation 39
Lofgren, Pastor Peter 106
Lower Saginaw 26, 28, 30
Lumbering
  End of 131
  Labor Unrest 84
  Sawmills 42-43
Lumbermen 85, 87
Lumbertown Enterprise 57-58
Lumbertown Entertainments 57

M
Madison Park 61
Maier, A. R., Drugstore 145
Manley, James 83
Manufacturing 131
Marsac, Joseph F. 22
Masho, Louis 23
Mason, Gov. Stevens T. 26
Masonic Temple 128
Mastodons 12
McCormick, William R. 18. 20, 30, 44
McCormick, J. J. 90
McCraney, Marshal D. H. 64, 71
McDermott, Terry 200
McEwan, John 91
McEwan, William 91
McGraw, John 30, 55, 178
McGraw's Sawmill 42, 61
McGraw, Thomas 87
Meeker and Adams, Grocery 60
Meisel, Albert E. 167
Mercy Hospital 78
Meredith, MI. 64
Michigan Central RR 55, 191
Michigan Haus 33

Michigan National Guard, 33rd Inf. 168-69
Michigan Sugar 146
Midland Street 86
Miller, Judge Albert 26, 44, 178
Missisauga Indians 18
Mix, Horace B. 82
Monitor Sugar Co. 112-23, 146
Moundbuilders 1-3
Movie Houses 180-81
Munger, MI. 116
Munger, A. S. 54-55
Muskegon, MI. 131

N
Natco Trucks 148
National Cycle Co. 148-49
Native Americans
  Agriculture 14-15
  Burning Practices 14-15
  Fishing 14-15
  Hunting 14-16
  Regional Adaptation 13
  Smallpox 28
  White Influence on 16-17
Nayanquing 19
Neering Hardware 60
Neighborhoods 39
Nelson, Neal, Family 106
Nevitt, Garland 198
North American Chemical Co. 132
Northwestern Gas & Pipe 47
Nouvel, Henri 18
Noyes, L. E. 91
Nuffer's General Store 143

O
O-ge-ma Ke-ga-to, (Chief Ogemaw) 22
Ojibwa Indians 21
Oswald, Peter J. 158

P
Paleoindian Culture 12
Panic of 1837 26
Parades 182-83
Parsons, Myra 80, 113, 126
Parsons, Mahlon E. 113
Partridge, Gen. Benjamin F. 82-83
Pawlaczyk Family 101
Phoenix Bldg. 59
Pinconning, MI. 14, 15, 116
Pine Forest 34
Plum, W. L. 178
Police 71-73, 184
Polish 61, 93-95, 100-101
Politics in Bay City 154-58
Political Parties 154
Politics, Ward System 155
Pontiac, Chief 14

Portsmouth 26, 58-59
Post Office 158-59
Prahl, Earl 19, 27
Presidential Yacht 135
Prestolite 148-151, 189
Primeau, Joseph 98
Progressive Party 157
Prohibition 172, 176-77
Prostitution 64
Putz's Hardware 97, 144

Q
Quanicasse, MI. 19

R
Railroads
  Disasters 163
  Early Construction 54-55, 191-93
  Stations 192-93
Red Arrow Division 168-69, 186
Republican Party 187
Resistence Welding 148
Resorts and Dance Halls 64
Richies Drive-In 190
Ridotto Bldg 77
Riley, Steven 22
Roads in Bay Co. 31
Rogers, D. L. 201
Rogers, Elizabeth 80
Roosevelt Park 22
Rosenbury & Sons 141, 186

S
Sage, Henry W. 28, 30, 55, 59, 65, 81, 84, 87, 90, 178
Sage Library 81, 84
Sage Salt Works 44
Sage Sawmill 30, 43
Saginaw 131
  Derivation of Name 17, 19
  Rivalry with Bay City 31
Saginaw River 50-51, 58-59
Sauk Indians, Legend of 17-18
Salt Manufacturing 30, 44-45
Salzburg 30, 33, 44, 97, 102
Samaritan Hospital 79
Sawmills
  Injuries in 97
  Labor 92-93
  Routine 93
Schnettler Family 102, 103-04
Schools
  All Saints High 197
  Central High 124, 194-96
  Dolsen 99 125
  Farragut 124
  Handy High 194-96
  Riegel 122
  St. James High 195
  St. John's (Essexville) 200

  Second Ward 125
  Sims Academy 125
  Washington 122
  Wenona 120-21
  West Bay City High 169, 194
  Western High (Auburn) 194
Schoolcraft, Henry 26
Schmidt, Walter L. 19
Schutjes, Fr. H. T. H. 107
Scubeck, Jospeh 100
Seligman, "Little Jake" 178
Sievers, Rev. Ferdinand 33
Sharp, John H. and Family 112
Sharp, W. P. 52
Sharpe, Mary A. 123
Shearer, Mayor George H. 95, 154
Shearer Block 59
Shipbuilding 50-51, 48-49
Shoppenogons, Chief 10, 20
Sixteenth Michigan Infantry 82-83
Skull Island, Battle of 18
Smith, Jacob 22
Smith, Henry B. 81, 148
Snyder, G. R. 115
Sovereign, Otto E. 147
Sovereign, Vera J. 188
Sovereign, William J. 147
Spanish-American War 167-69
Sports 164-65
Squaconning Creek 15, 18
St. Laurent Bros. 98
St. Patrick's Day Parade 108
Staudacher Family 102
Staudacher, Les 200
Staudacher, Mentor 172
Steetcars 173
Sterling Homes 147
Storms 163
Strevel, Herman 187
Sugar Beet Manufacturing 112-13, 133, 146
Swart, Stephen 138
Swedish 61, 93, 113, 146

T
Talaga, Mark 197
Tamblyn, Marian 186
Tanner, Helen H. 17
Taylor, Ann Edson 200
Ten Hours or No Sawdust Strike, 95
Theaters 180-181
  Aladdin 181
  Alvarado 181
  Bijou 181
  Washington 180
  Westover Opera House 59
  Westown 181
  Woods Opera House 180

Tittabawassee River 19
Tobico Hunt Club 90
Tobico Marsh 19
Tocqueville, Alexis de 23, 27
Toeppner Bro's Carriages 144
Transportation 43
Tripp, Samuel J. 48
Trudell, John B. 23
Trombley, Gassette 20
Trombley House, See Center House
Trombley, Leon 23
Trombley, Louis 20
Trombley, Joseph 30
Trombley, Mader 26, 27
Tupper's Drugstore 143
Tupper, Dr. Virgil 78
Turner, Capt. George 82
Treaty of Saginaw (1819) 21-22
Twenties, The 76, 172

U
Unions 93
Union Truck 148, 150

V
Van Mullekom, Frank 107
Vukavich, Ann 187

W
Wages 93
Wakefield, Francis 17
War of 1812 20-22
Water Street 59
Watson, Jim 175
Wauless, Capt, George 73-75
Webster, Mary S. 123
Wells, C. R. 81
Wenona 19. 30, 58-59
Wenona Beach 173-75
Wenonah Park 166
West Bay City 58-59, 84
West Bay City Hospital 79
Wheeler, Frank W. 48-49
Whitney, C. C. 90
Wickes Bros. 43
Willard, See Ittner's Corner
Williams, Havey 53
Wilson Body Co. 171
Wirgowski, Dennis 199
Wood Products Industry 46
Woodenware 133
Wooden Pipe Manufacturing 47
World War I 168-71
World War II 186-87
World War II, Housing 187
Wright's, Dave, Cafe 175
Wright, Judge 88-89

207

Citizens Bank

The Citizen's Bank building at 701 Washington has quite an "electrifying" past. The building was originally constructed and used for many years by Consumers Power Company, as their district offices and retail sales building. In fact, the Bay City Daily Times did a whole section devoted to Consumers Power and their new office on February 11, 1931, one day before the three day grand opening extravaganza.

The building was actually started in April of 1930 and was originally slated to open in December of that year, but a few delays pushed back the opening to February of 1931. The building, which reportedly cost $300,000, was considered to be the "model of the company's district offices in various sections of the State." The property was acquired from G.W. Ames and the general contractor was the Henry C. Weber Construction Company. It was designed by Allied Engineers, Inc. an affiliate of Consumers Power, to be an "attractive form of colonial architecture that is being used in office buildings of that size and larger in many sections of the country."

As for the building, it was originally built with three floors and a basement, but had a foundation built strong enough to allow the expansion of at least three more floors. The brick, stone and concrete construction supposedly made the building fire proof. Many local firms had a hand in the building of this office. The Westover-Kamm Company did most of the interior mill work. Meisel Hardware Supply Company provided the general hardware. Roofing was done by Valley Roofing Company. The interior decorating was completed by The Bay City Decorating Company. The cement was provided by Aetland Portland Cement Company.

While much of the construction was by local firms, the building materials list had a much broader scope. The granite was from Vermont. Marble-Tavertine was brought in from Georgia. Tavernell from Tennessee was also used. Terrazzino chips were imported from Italy. The face brick was from Ohio clay. Terra Cotta was molded by artists form New York. Even the special insulating and acoustical material was made from cane brake grown in the reclaimed everglades of Florida.

The building was used by Consumers Power Company in one capacity or another from 1931 until sometime in 1974. Second Nationsl Bank opened for business on January 5, 1976 and completely renovated the building's main floor. In 1996, Second National Bank changed their name to Citizens Bank and the building continued to hold the offices of "power," not electrical, but financial.

Top left: This photo, dated May 16, 1930, shows the foundation of the Consumers Power Company office building under construction.

Top right: Exterior of the Consumers Power Company offices, prior to its completion in 1931.

Left: Interior photo of a portion of the first floor of the newly opened Consumers Power Company offices. This photo was taken some time in 1931.

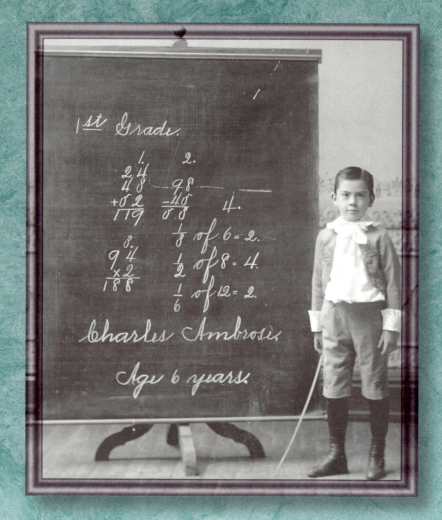

Charles Ambrose
Age 6 years.